SINGLE EUROPE,
SINGLE IRELAND?

Single Europe, Single Ireland?

Uneven Development in Process

JAMES GOODMAN

University of Technology, Sydney,
Australia and Open University,
Milton Keynes, England

IRISH ACADEMIC PRESS
DUBLIN • PORTLAND, OR

First published in 2000 by
IRISH ACADEMIC PRESS
44, Northumberland Road, Dublin 4, Ireland
and in the United States of America by
IRISH ACADEMIC PRESS
c/o ISBS, 5804 NE Hassalo Street, Portland, OR 97213–3644

website: www.iap.ie

© James Goodman 2000

British Library Cataloguing in Publication Data
Goodman, James
    Single Europe, single Ireland? Uneven development in process
    1. Ireland – Economic integration   2. Ireland – Economic conditions –
    1949– – Regional disparities
    I. Title
    330. 9'415'082
    ISBN 0–7165–2646–8 hardback
    ISBN 0–7165–2647–6 paperback

Library of Congress Cataloguing-in-Publication Data
Goodman, James, 1965–
    Single Europe, single Ireland? Uneven development in process /
    James Goodman.
        p. cm.
    Includes bibliographical references and index.
    ISBN 0–7165–2646–8 (hbk.)—ISBN 0–7165–2647–6 (pbk.)
    1. Ireland—Relations—Northern Ireland.   2. Northern Ireland—
    Politicals and government—1994–   3. Ireland—Politics and
    government—1949–   4. Northern Ireland—Economics conditions.
    5. Northern Ireland—Relations—Ireland.   6. Ireland—Economic
    conditions—1949–   7. Europe—Economic integration.   8. Irish
    unification question.   I. Title.
    DA964.N67G66   2000
    303.48'24150416—dc21
                                                                99–28734
                                                                    CIP

Typeset in 10.5 pt on 12 pt Palatino by
Carrigboy Typesetting Services, County Cork
Printed by
Creative Print and Design (Wales), Ebbw Vale

Contents

Tables and figures

List of Abbreviations

AIA	Anglo-Irish Agreement
AIIC	Anglo-Irish Inter-Governmental Council
CAP	Common Agricultural Policy
CBI	Confederation of British Industry
CII	Confederation of Irish Industry
CSCE	Conference on Security and Cooperation in Europe
DUP	Democratic Unionist Party
EAGGF	European Agriculture Guidance and Guarantee Fund
ECU	European Currency Units
EEC	European Economic Community
EMU	Economic and Monetary Union
EP	European Parliament
EPC	European Political Cooperation
ERDF	European Regional Development Fund
ERM	Exchange Rate Mechanism
ESF	European Social Fund
EU	European Union
FEA	Fair Employment Agency
GATT	General Agreement on Tariffs and Trade
GDP	Gross Domestic Product
GNP	Gross National Product
ICTU	Irish Congress of Trade Unions
IDA	Industrial Development Authority
IDB	Industrial Development Board
IRA	Irish Republican Army
ITB	Irish Trade Board
LEDU	Local Enterprise Development Board
MEP	Member of the European Parliament
NESC	National Economic and Social Council
NICE	Northern Ireland Centre in Europe
NIEC	Northern Ireland Economic Council

NIF	New Ireland Forum
NIHE	Northern Ireland Housing Executive
NILP	Northern Ireland Labour Party
NIO	Northern Ireland Office
OECD	Organisation for Economic Cooperation and Development
OEEC	Organisation of European Economic Cooperation
PUP	Protestant Unionist Party
RUC	Royal Ulster Constabulary
SDLP	Social Democratic and Labour Party
SEA	Single European Act
SEM	Single European Market
UDA	Ulster Defence Association
UDR	Ulster Defence Regimen
UUP	Ulster Unionist Party
UVF	Ulster Volunteer Force

Acknowledgements

This book has its origins in friendships and political involvements dating from the early 1980s. It also reflects an academic journey through London, Milton Keynes, Belfast and now Sydney; through a Master's dissertation, a PhD thesis and subsequent years of post-doctoral research. I would like to thank those who have encouraged me to persist with this writing, especially Robbie McVeigh and Conor Shields in Belfast, Rosemary Sales in London, James Anderson in Newcastle-upon-Tyne and Rowena Lennox in Sydney. I would also like to thank the Open University, Milton Keynes, and the University of Technology, Sydney, for funding the research on which this book is based.

James Goodman
Sydney, January 1999

Foreword

It seems clear that Ireland is now undergoing a major political and socio-economic transition that has been unmatched in scale and intensity by any period since 1880–1920. The latter period laid the foundation for the partition of Ireland, the current period is undoing most of the key elements of the partition settlement albeit not in the manner envisaged by traditional anti-partitionists. James Goodman's book makes an important contribution to our understanding of this emergent Ireland. It will stimulate debate, not least in its challenge to those who have failed to recognise the dynamics of change and who persist in fighting old battles over redundant forms of territorial sovereignty.

Liam O'Dowd
Professor of Sociology,
Queen's University,
Belfast June 1999

Preface

The national conflict in Ireland has its origins in uneven development under British colonialism. The conflict has created and feeds off sharp divisions between the island's North and South. There is a history of diverging socio-economic interests, conflicting ideological positions and divided institutions. Against these historical legacies and on-going realities, there are intensifying pressures for more 'even' development. Socio-economic, ideological and institutional divisions are in the process of being reversed and the European Union is playing a key role in this. The EU integration process is stimulating an Irish integration process, so that by the end of the 1990s the need for stronger linkages between North and South has almost reached the status of conventional wisdom.

Single Europe, Single Ireland? analyses the process of reversing the uneven development. The first chapter provides a historical account of the conflict, emphasising its North–South dimensions. This provides an essential backdrop to discussions of socio-economic interests, party-political positions and state policies, North and South. Across these issue areas, the process of EU integration is linked to the wider process of convergence in Ireland. This is set against continuing divisions and divergences, leading to the conclusion in the book that North–South linkages require concerted state action and guidance.

Both Ireland and Europe are divided in their unity, a paradox that can only be reconciled through common initiatives that bridge national jurisdictions. The intensifying debate about such initiatives is of central importance for the economic and political future of Ireland. This book closes with the 1998 'Peace Agreement' and in many ways it offers an interpretation of the historical context that made that Agreement a possibility. The partition of Ireland's economic interests, party politics and state structures has been challenged 'from within';

the Peace Agreement potentially allows parties and governments to set about deconstructing the North–South divisions that have fuelled the conflict.

Introduction:
interests, ideologies
and institutions

European Union (EU) states have responded to globalised economic power by jointly pursuing national interests within the EU 'global region'. Across the EU, the nature of political authority has changed as states have fused national and regional frameworks for regulation. A range of policy frameworks and representative bodies have emerged that no longer operate according to the dictates of national state-centred politics. The shape and power of these non-state bodies is dictated by the need to influence globalised economic forces and they cut across existing state boundaries, disrupting state powers and state-centred nationalisms. In doing so, they perhaps offer a pathway out of monolithic, mythical conceptions of 'national' state sovereignty.

This has profound implications for Ireland, where the political demands of business élites, the ideological conflict between political parties and the policies pursued by the British and Irish states are to a degree being forced into an all-island regional framework. Across the EU, tensions between national and regional dynamics are opening up new opportunities for institutional change. In Ireland they are stimulating debates about possible North–South institutions – debates that are of central importance both for the economic and for the political future of the island.

At the same time, the EU is divided in its unity. Reflecting the weakness of a transnational Euro-identity, EU integration is largely confined to economic concerns rather than social, cultural or political matters. This generates sharp disjunctures between a growing transnationalism in economic affairs and

1

the continuing ideological significance of national and state divisions. Integration may strengthen non-national regional bodies, but EU treaties are founded on national politics and in many respects strengthen state powers. States dominate EU decision-making and have retained direct control over many areas of social life, and as they respond differently to the integration process there can be 'divergence' as well as 'convergence' between states.

This is a particular problem in Ireland which is divided by differing British and Irish policies. For the first twenty years of EU membership the fault-line between 'EU-sceptic' and 'EU-enthusiast' has been inscribed across the North of Ireland, the EU's only land border with the UK. Many of the hoped for benefits of the EU hinge on the ability to overcome these divergences and to construct a regional 'system of regulation' for Ireland, North and South. This in turn depends on the emergence of more coherent, all-Ireland institutions with executive powers and democratic accountability.

Conflicts between pan-European integration and national division are a general feature of EU politics, and in Ireland they are particularly sharply defined. The two parts of Ireland are converging along a common development path as both become highly, even exceptionally, integrated into the EU's 'global region'. Against this, the dispute over national state sovereignty between unionists and nationalists and between British and Irish state sovereignty dominates political life in the North. Irish nationalists and republicans contest Northern Ireland's constitutional status as part of the UK, while Ulster unionists and loyalists seek to defend it against incorporation into the Irish Republic. The juxtaposition between these national divisions and increased integration into the EU poses sharp dilemmas for political actors, North and South, and is becoming a defining factor in political development.

This book examines these issues along three strands of analysis, focusing on interest based conflicts, ideological conflicts and disputes over public institutions:

- conflicts of interest are largely defined in economic terms as expressed in conflicts between business, labour and other organised groupings;

- discussion of ideological conflict centres on disputes between political parties, for instance over questions of development and nationalism;
- analysis of policy conflicts focuses on state institutions and their interaction with sub-national and pan-European institutions.

This approach is derived from Gramscian theories of socio-political change, developed by theorists of global politics, such as Robert Cox, who argue that cross-national integration creates sharp tensions within and across national societies (Gramsci, 1971; Cox, 1987). Economic forces and associated interests become increasingly globalised, but ideological and institutional relations remain largely orientated to the national state. Institutions, ideologies and interests are highly interdependent and mismatches between them can create sharp discontinuities. Ideological compromises forged through the national state, for instance, may be disrupted and undermined as economic interests move outside the national framework.

The three-part framework offers a means of understanding the tensions generated by EU integration and their implications for nationalisms and national conflict. The process of creating a transnational economic space within the EU unavoidably spills over into national politics and state policy-making. Integration can make a nonsense of distinctions between 'low' and 'high' politics and between 'domestic' and 'foreign', and in the process can realign state sovereignties and nationalisms. With the emergence of a transnational economic sphere, nationally defined interests seek new frameworks for accumulation and regulation often in separation from existing state structures. This imposes new priorities on political parties and has the effect of repositioning or redefining states and nationalisms, opening up new avenues for institutional and ideological change.

This book explores these avenues, arguing that they help to explain the emergence of peace-making agendas in Ireland during the 1990s. The book is a discussion of transnational integration and offers an interpretation of the factors that led to the 1998 Peace Agreement. But it is also an intervention into debates about the nature of nationalism. The book analyses nationalism as a political ideology rooted in various forms of spatial division, categorised into divisions of interests, ideologies and institutions. This emphasis on spatial divisions is largely derived from the work of Tom Nairn and in particular from his book, *The Break-up of Britain*, published in 1977, and from its sequel, *Faces of Nationalism: Janus Revisited*, published in 1997.

For Nairn, nationalism is a necessary outcome of capitalism; its 'real origins are . . . located not in the folk, not in the individual's repressed passion for some sort of wholeness or identity, but in the machinery of world political economy' (Nairn, 1977, p. 335). Nationalism is not chosen as the vehicle for political change but is imposed by the logic of uneven capitalist development. In this sense nationalism expresses the fact of territoriality in class relations, that paradoxically results from the globalising spread and deepening reach of capitalism. The prediction of 'liberal' thinkers on international politics that global commerce would lead to global social harmony could not have been more mistaken. The national state was and remains the central means of gaining some autonomy in the global economy, and for Nairn it is the main way for people to 'contest the concrete form in which . . . 'progress' had taken them by the throat' (Nairn, 1977, p. 337–9).

This interpretation of nationalism has strong resonances in Ireland. Uneven cultural and economic development between northern and southern Ireland is cited by a number of commentators as the central factor in the emergence of unionist–nationalist conflict in the late nineteenth century and in the construction of Partition.[1] Partly reflecting this, some Northern unionist politicians talk of the 'two nations' of Ireland, while Irish nationalists have often emphasised the on-going linkages that may override North–South uneven development. Against unionist insistence on the naturalness and permanence of Partition, nationalists stress the possibility of a transition to more 'even' development, that will in time undermine political divisions on the island.

In 1977 and 1997 Tom Nairn firmly supported the unionist-orientated 'two nations' model. For him, the United Kingdom was breaking up into four components – England, Wales, Scotland and Northern Ireland. The main motor for the break-up was uneven development and in the Irish case this was a double unevenness, not only between Northern Ireland and Britain, but also between Northern Ireland and the independent Southern Irish state, the Republic of Ireland. For Nairn, Northern industrialisation during the nineteenth century had 'permanently' separated it from 'the history of Catholic, under-developed Southern Ireland' (1977, p. 235). This required the emergence of an autonomous Northern Ireland nationalism, and the formation of an eventually independent Northern Ireland state.

In 1977 Nairn cited the 1974 'Protestant general strike' as marking a turning point in Northern Ireland politics. The stoppage persuaded the British government to abandon the power-sharing Sunningdale Agreement which had been signed with liberal unionists, Northern nationalists and the Southern government. For Nairn, this clearly marked 'where the centre of political gravity lies in any farther developments' (1977, p. 241). In 1997 he pointed to unionist opposition to the 1995 Framework Document, which later was reflected in the 1998 Peace Agreement. For him the proposals had an 'emphasis . . . much more on the cross-border authorities than on the new government in Belfast', and added that 'unionists have not misread this and are right to object . . . by threatening to bring down the Major government at Westminster' (1997, p. 163).

In both 1977 and 1997 unionist intransigence was welcomed as an unchanging and unchangeable political fact. For Nairn, unionists were right to defend their distinctiveness against the Southern state, and against Irish nationalists. They were also right to resist the imposition of British policy, and were encouraged to assert their own right to statehood, autonomous from both Britain and the Republic. These interpretations ignore the unionist desire for Northern Ireland to remain part of Britain and not to form an independent state (Boyce, 1993). They also ignore the sectarian foundations of Northern Ireland, thereby failing to acknowledge that it could never form the basis for a stable unified 'nation', least of all an independent entity (Gallagher, 1990).

But more fundamentally, in asserting the permanence of unionism and the necessity for Northern Ireland statehood, Nairn is in conflict with his own assertion that nationalism is not an essential characteristic of 'the folk', but a product of the 'machinery of world political economy'. Nationalisms are not permanent or fixed but are contingent formations subject to the shifts and turns of political economy. Uneven development between northern and southern Ireland, whether socio-economic, ideological or institutional, was a central factor in the emergence of unionism and in the island's eventual partition. But there is no reason then to assume that North–South divisions and the resulting political alignments are in any sense permanent. On the contrary, there is plentiful evidence that uneven development has gone into reverse.

This book analyses this evidence, focusing on the impacts of European integration, and asking whether the formation of a 'single Europe' is leading to the emergence of a 'single Ireland'. There are four main chapters. The first gives some historical analysis, assessing the competing historical pressures for convergence and divergence between northern and southern Ireland. Using the analytical framework outlined above, it focuses on economic interests, party politics and state policy. It is argued that the conflict emerged out of uneven development between North and South, which was exploited by British nationalists and their allies in the North. Nairn's view that this requires the creation of an independent Northern Ireland is rejected. Instead, three contrasting conclusions are drawn – that North–South uneven development has proved to be short-lived; North and South divisions have become an obstacle to development, and all-Ireland institutions are required to overcome these divisions and to express pan-Irish configurations.

The ensuing three chapters examine more contemporary tendencies, stressing the role of the EU in encouraging the reversal of uneven development. Each chapter counterposes the pressures for convergence, on an all-Ireland regional basis, against pressures for 'national' state-centred divergence. There are sharp North–South divisions between Northern and Southern economies, between unionists and nationalists and between the British and the Irish states. Yet these divisions are undermined by pressures for North–South economic integration, by the emergence of an island-wide framework for ideological conflict and by the creation of North–South institutions.

Chapter Two maps out shifting economic interests, suggesting that EU integration encourages the formation, or perhaps reformation, of an all-Ireland bourgeoisie. There are tensions between Northern and Southern–based business classes – tensions which reflect the divided state sectors and the economic legacy of political division. But these have increasingly been overlaid by new common interests, most clearly expressed in lobbying by Northern business groupings.

Chapter Three analyses associated redefinitions of party politics, arguing that a pan-Irish frame for ideological conflict has emerged. In part this is precipitated by the process of European integration, and is contradicted by on-going and sometimes intensified conflict over questions of national sovereignty.

Chapter Four discusses the changing framework for state and public policy. This again has been caught in a tension between all-Ireland regionalising pressures and national state division, for instance, between joint North–South EU funding frameworks and the conflicting British–Irish claims to jurisdiction in the North.

In terms of scope, the historical analysis begins with pressures for north–south divergence dating from the repression of the United Irishmen in 1798. The account ends with the ceasefire announced by the Irish Republican Army (IRA) in 1994 and the ensuing 'peace process'. In the conclusions there is some discussion of the Anglo–Irish Framework Documents of 1995, and the 1998 Peace Agreement, but for the most part analysis is deliberately prepeace process. This is partly to avoid the range of contingent factors that have come into play with the transition to relatively peaceful political debates on the future of Northern Ireland. Analysis is restricted to the longer-term tendencies that emerged despite the military conflict, rather than because of its cessation. Official documents and secondary material are used to develop the historical analysis while the successive accounts of more contemporary developments draw on a survey of newspapers and official publications to the end of August 1994.

1

Historical roots: North–South division and conflict

This chapter begins with a short account of North–South divergence and national conflict in Ireland, from the 1801 Act of Union to Partition in 1921, focusing on uneven development and socio-economic divergence in the late nineteenth century. This is followed by a more in-depth analysis examining North–South convergence in the mid to late twentieth century. It is argued that North–South division in Ireland emerged out of three complementary developments: first, a combination of uneven economic development and sectarianism in the labour market; second, political action by Unionists and Nationalists; and third, state policy. Discussion of the pressures for North–South convergence thus focuses on the degree to which there has been a reversal of uneven development and an associated removal of sectarian labour relations; a realignment of political consciousness and associated political action by social and political actors, North and South; and a reorientation of state policies to express increased North–South convergence.

Nineteenth-century Irish history is dominated by sharp economic decline over much of the island, except in parts of the north, which became highly industrialised. The 1801 Act of Union, which was imposed after the 'United Irishmen' had been repressed, integrated the relatively weak Irish economy into the circuit of British-based capital and led to industrial collapse and rural depopulation across much of Ireland (Murray, 1903, p. 416). Free trade under the Act gave British exporters unlimited access to the Irish economy, while monetary union between Sterling and emerging Irish currencies, also in 1801, systematically constrained Irish growth patterns. At the same time, domestic Irish purchasing power was undermined by

British taxation policy. Before the union, Ireland contributed £2.5 million in taxes to the British Treasury. After the two taxation systems were merged in 1817, this doubled to £5 million and by 1896, Ireland was contributing £7 million despite a halving of the Irish population over the same period (due to emigration and the mid-century famine) (Murray 1903, p. 399; Strauss, 1951).

The result was a process of 'arrested development' (Riordan, 1920, p. 280). The depression of the mid 1820s, which immediately followed the removal of tariff protection for the Irish cotton industry, led to the closure of half the cotton factories in Ireland; similarly, woollen producers were reduced to ten per cent of the Irish market (Cullen, 1972, p. 13). Where British products penetrated the local economy, British railway capital followed, with an extensive railway building programme, linking all the major garrison towns by 1855 and adding a further one hundred miles by the 1870s (Lee, 1973). When the world economy entered the next slump (in the mid 1870s), industries producing consumer goods, which had to some extent re-established themselves, were particularly affected as cheaply produced British goods flooded into the now easily accessible Irish market.

The destruction of all but the sturdiest sectors of southern industry from the 1820s was paralleled by an expansion in commercial agriculture, on the back of increased British corn prices. This fuelled a rapid growth in rural population and led to extensive subdivision of landholdings (Kennedy, 1988). With the abolition of the Corn Laws (1846) and rising British beef prices, exports of livestock rose 600 per cent between 1820 and 1870 after 160 years of relative stability (Mjoset, 1993, p. 215). Landowners converted land holdings into vast tracts of pasture that some have likened to the Latin American 'latifundi' (Probert, 1978). By 1850, the amount of smallholdings in Ireland had been halved and dispossessed tenants flocked to northern Irish and British towns to find work. In the 1860s, one tenth of the navvies in Britain and a quarter of the population of Liverpool were Irish (Hunt 1981); many others emigrated to the US, while those left behind filled the workhouses (in 1851 there were 102,818 people in Irish workhouses). Later in the nineteenth century, an international depression in the prices of agricultural produce (the price of beef fell by a third between 1876 and 1885) and the progressive penetration of British meat and dairy markets by overseas competitors once again undermined the Irish economy: the total value of agricultural exports from Ireland to Britain fell by a third and again the pace of Irish emigration increased (Solow, 1971, p. 171).

For much of the nineteenth century, and into the twentieth, the Irish economy had become dependent on highly unstable British markets for agricultural products – an 'entirely inadequate . . . sheet anchor for the Irish economy' (Strauss, 1951, p. 174). With domestic industry unable to provide new jobs and emigration failing even to supply a short-term solution to rural poverty, the demand for a more equitable spread of landownership became the dominant political issue. Reflecting the distorted nature of the Irish economy, this 'struggle to retain control of the land for those who worked it' (Mitchell, 1974) pivoted on a class alliance between an impoverished tenant class and an Irish middle class concerned with protecting the Irish economy from British exports. Thirty years of pressure for Catholic emancipation, after the 1801 Act of Union, had radicalised a Catholic middle class and placed it at the forefront of Irish nationalism. This was fuelled by the disestablishment of the Church of Ireland in 1868, the growth in Catholic-run education from 1879 and a three-fold expansion in the Catholic clergy, leading to a rapid spread of English literacy. Simultaneously, rent strikes against absentee landlords through the 'Land League' led to evictions by the British army and quickly developed into a more explicitly nationalist movement through the 'Home Rule League'. Dispossessed rural tenantry, a growing Catholic clergy and an urban middle class joined together in an a conservative nationalist alliance, expressed in the Irish Parliamentary Party.

Attempts at addressing rural discontent and defusing Irish nationalism through the Wyndham Acts, failed to prevent the emergence of a more urban and working–class national movement in the early part of the twentieth century. This movement was linked to Republican demands for an end to British domination of Irish culture, administration and politics, and was further radicalised by the British repression of the 1916 uprising. The Republican party, Sinn Féin, founded in 1905, began to receive mass support in the wake of an anti-conscription campaign; with the 1918 election, Sinn Féin increased its representation in the 103–seat Irish Parliament from seven to seventy-three members. There followed three years of armed conflict between British forces and the IRA defending the 'Underground Republic'. During this time, Sinn Féin support was confirmed, in council, county and parliamentary elections, and by 1921 the party occupied 130 of the Parliament's 180 seats. The war of independence ended with the creation of the Irish Free State in 1921, with 'Dominion' status similar to Canada, leading to the 1921–23 civil war between pro-Treaty and anti-Treaty factions of the Republican movement.

This pattern of industrial decline, rural poverty, middle-class alienation and revolution against the British state did not extend to the whole of Ireland in the nineteenth century. Industry in northern Irish towns resisted competition from large British producers, and by the end of the nineteenth century, the region had become the world's largest producer of linen and possessed the world's largest shipyard (owned by Harland and Wolff). Explanations of this uneven development have been hotly contested, not least because of their contemporary implications. Leaving aside sectarian arguments that the Protestant communities of northern Ireland possessed a higher level of business acumen than their Catholic counterparts (see Rosebaum, 1912), three broad explanations can be identified. The first centres on what is said to be a unique structure of land-holding in Northern Ireland which, it is argued, granted Protestant tenants security of tenure and fair rents – an 'Ulster custom' that contrasted with conditions elsewhere in Ireland where there was little or no security of tenure (Probert, 1978; Boserup, 1972, p. 159). This view has been challenged on the basis that the so-called 'custom' made very little difference in practice, not least because agricultural land in Northern Ireland was peculiarly non-productive (Solow, 1971, p. 31).

A second explanation focuses on the labour market in the north which, it is argued, allowed the super-exploitation of 'unskilled' labour. While 'skilled' work in textiles, ship-building and engineering attracted wage rates significantly higher even than equivalent jobs elsewhere in the UK, wage rates for unskilled occupations were driven well below the worst UK rates of pay (Bell, 1987; Patterson, 1980; Armstrong, 1951). This reflected sectarianised labour markets in the north, combined with large inflows of unskilled labour from the south. Forced off the land, labour flocked to the cities and Belfast grew from a small town of 20,000 in 1835 to a city of 100,000 by 1850, with the fastest growth during the linen boom which coincided with the decline of tillage in favour of pasture on the land. The middle classes and the skilled labouring classes, dominated by Protestants, were able to restrict access to occupational and professional privilege, and were relatively insulated from this reserve army of migrant labour – unlike unskilled Protestants and Catholics. The result was sharp social inequalities in the north, with skilled workers being paid a third more than their counterparts in Britain, and unskilled workers a third less (Murray, 1903, p. 416; Hunt, 1981, p. 171).[1] With overall labour costs kept well below British levels, the interlocking of sectarianism and industrialism became the central, structural precondition of uneven development.

One problem with this approach is that the southern towns also experienced an influx of migrant labour willing to work for low wages. This points to the possibility that the north's middle class was particularly well placed, geographically and socially, to take advantage of these labour market conditions. This third explanation centres on the uneven access to overseas markets, via Glasgow and Liverpool, and to sources of British-based finance. As Irish cotton manufacturers lost their domestic markets to British producers, those in the north reinvested to produce linen for international markets, particularly in the USA. The industry was organically tied to British trade routes – in 1861, seventy-five per cent of Irish linen was exported, seventy per cent to the USA. The 'cotton famine' caused by the American Civil War accentuated this dependence as linen exports expanded from £6 million to £10 million in the space of one year (1863–4) and employment rose to 57,000 by 1876, peaking at 69,000 in the 1890s. This rapidly expanding linen industry, centred on Belfast, gained economies in handling, insurance and finance that were not available elsewhere in Ireland, and Belfast became Ireland's entrepôt. By 1900, two-thirds of Ireland's exports were routed through the city, boosting shipbuilding and machine production, which expanded to employ 30,000 people by 1915, supplying ships primarily for British mercantile capital.

However uneven development is explained, there can be little doubt that it led to the creation of a northern bourgeoisie linked to British capital. While Belfast was dominated by the shipbuilding and linen industries, the rest of Ireland was left behind. In 1890, shipbuilders, linen magnates and the export-oriented elite of Belfast jointly employed thirty-five per cent of the northern workforce, contrasting with the southern bourgeoisie which directly employed only thirteen per cent of the southern workforce, primarily in food processing and distribution tied to Irish internal markets (with Dublin brewing as the exception) (Kennedy, 1988, p. 8). Dependence on British trade routes and British sources of finance bound the interests of northern capital to British political parties and industrialists, as opposed to a much weaker southern bourgeoisie concerned to protect its potential industrial base in the face of overseas competition.

The class interests of northern workers were also inter-woven with the politics of nationalism and unionism. As Belfast's Catholic population increased from 10 per cent in 1800 to thirty-three per cent in 1850 and forty-three per cent by the end of the 1860s, Protestant patronage gained a heightened significance (Pringle, 1985, p. 11; Gibbon, 1975, p. 96; Rumpf and Hepburn, 1977). Relations between patron and client became the key to gaining employment in the cities; the Orange Order, which had played a central role in repressing the United Irishmen and for some years had been in decline, re-emerged to act as an employment agency for migrant Protestants bearing 'Certificates of Character' from their landlords (Pringle, 1985, p. 209; Gibbon, 1975, p. 16; Buckland, 1973, p. 22; Boserup, 1972, p. 16).

Meanwhile, inter-communal competition between less-advantaged Protestants and Catholics boiled over into a 'whole series of riots' that transformed the nature of politics in Northern Ireland (Rumpf and Hepburn, 1977, p. 165). From the 1850s, these sectarian riots became less localised and more segregated along occupational fault-lines and rioting became a political act with deep roots in the dual labour market that was emerging in Belfast's linen and shipbuilding industries. Skilled Protestant workers from the new shipyards and engineering factories quickly became the élite of anti-nationalist extremism, expressing emerging political divisions in the unevenly developed Ireland of the nineteenth century. Riots in 1864, for instance, on the day a statue was dedicated to O'Connell in Dublin, led to the first attempts at expelling Catholic labour from Belfast's shipyards. After similar riots during the 1892–3 Home Rule crisis, Harland and Wolff sacked 190 of the 225 Catholic workers and the remainder were expelled in 1912 (Goldring, 1991, p. 61).

Hastened by the Home Rule crises of 1886 and 1896, the new variant of working-class unionism became aligned with the increasingly strident unionism of the northern bourgeoisie. This political alliance between workers, tenants, factory owners and landlords was expressed in the Ulster Unionist Party, which was founded in 1912 and gave political force to the logic of uneven economic and social development that had been etched into Irish society. This sharply contrasted with the South, where rural discontent had combined with demands for protectionism to create a nationalist movement aspiring to self-determination and national independence from the British state (Strauss, 1951). These patterns of uneven socio-economic and political development, north and south, were to some degree reversed in the mid-twentieth century. This is examined in what follows, first by analysing socio-economic interests, then political conflict and state policies.

1.1 SOCIO-ECONOMIC INTERESTS

Divergence between the north and south in Ireland during the nineteenth century was to facilitate and legitimise the British decision to impose Partition in 1921. Jurisdictional division only exaggerated the divergence; during the 1930s and 1940s, the South pursued a relatively autarchic, separate development path, while the North sought greater integration with the British economy. But by the 1950s, the two economies had shifted into reverse gear as they exhausted the benefits of these separate strategies.

In response, both North and South sought to attract multinational investment, leading to a rapid reorientation of economic development from heavy producer industry in the North and from agricultural commerce in the South to mutual dependence on externally owned, consumer-orientated manufacturing industry. The weakening of this strategy in Northern Ireland during the 1970s and 1980s, largely due to institutional inflexibility and political conflict, led to renewed economic divergence. This persisted until the 1990s, when mutual integration into the Single European Market (SEM) began to offer a new agenda for North–South convergence. This subsection examines these economic shifts and associated socio-economic interests.

North–South convergence

Nineteenth century economic divergence between north and south was exaggerated by Partition and was sustained until the 1950s when a process of North–South economic convergence began to emerge. The nineteenth century had seen the growth of an indigenous industrial base in the north, but deep interdependencies between the three leading sectors of the northern Irish economy – linen, engineering and shipbuilding – made it particularly vulnerable to structural shifts in the world economy. Even in the 1890s, the linen industry in Northern Ireland was 'capturing a larger share of a declining market' and fifty years later, both the linen and the shipbuilding industries were facing terminal decline (Cullen, 1972, p. 159). At the same time, conditions on the periphery of the British economy rendered Northern Ireland incapable of diversifying its highly vulnerable industrial base. There were two reasons for this.

First, there were labour market constraints. As noted earlier, high rates of pay for skilled labour and low rates of pay for unskilled labour had been a feature of the economy since the mid-nineteenth century. In the 1950s, skilled workers could expect to receive the same wage rate whether in Belfast or London, while the rates of pay for unskilled workers remained 'consistently below' the lowest UK rates (within the fifteen lowest paid sectors of industry regulated by Wages Councils;

Stormont, 1957, p. 225). This pattern still existed in the early 1960s when fitters in Belfast were being paid at the same rate as their counterparts in London, while labourers received a lower wage than any labourer in Coventry, Birmingham or London (Stormont, 1962, Appendix 1). Northern Protestants maintained a relatively secure domination of skilled occupations, with thirty-four per cent of all Protestants in Northern Ireland employed as skilled labourers in 1911 (the corresponding figure for Catholics was twenty-four per cent). This short-circuited militant trade unionism and maintained stability in the unionist class alliance.

But when the shipbuilding and linen industries collapsed in the 1950s, sectarian division became a liability, as industry was unable to reorientate itself to changing conditions without challenging the job security of its largely Protestant skilled workforce. The 'new wave' industries, of chemical engineering, synthetic fibres and electrical engineering required a labour process that did not rely on the 'skilled' labour of a minority of employees, and by 1971, only nineteen per cent of Protestants were skilled labourers (seventeen per cent of Catholics) (Bew, 1979, p. 167). This was partially resolved by an increase in white-collar employment but there were many less skilled, less well-connected Protestant workers who lost out, thereby destabilising the unionist political bloc.

Second, there were financial constraints. Without access to a large local market, industry lacked a guaranteed rate of profit and was unable to finance reinvestment. The structure of banking and finance, together with the deficit on the trade balance with Britain, ensured that Northern Ireland capital was constantly drained off into the wider UK economy. Most of Northern industry was privately owned (sixty per cent in the 1950s as compared with thirty-six per cent in the UK) and hence was dependent upon Northern financial markets, which were rarely in a position to create the required credit (Stormont, 1957). This provided an almost watertight guarantee that the northern economy would be unable to modernise itself: despite a steep growth in British government expenditure in Northern Ireland, rising by 600 per cent between 1946 and 1963, capital flows into the region were dwarfed by capital outflows; in 1950 for instance, capital exports stood at £330 million and capital imports at £85 million (Stormont, 1957). The result was under-investment in both existing and new capital ventures, leading to falling productivity. Capital formation slumped by over a third in the 1950s and British based multinational companies such as ICI, Viyella and Courtaulds sidelined the declining linen industry and invested in labour shedding synthetic fibres. As a result, there was a twenty-eight per cent cut in manufacturing employment, ten per cent more than in Britain between 1950 and 1961, and unemployment rose to 7.8 per cent while in Britain it remained at 1.8 per cent (Stormont 1962, p. 70). Together, these political and economic factors stimulated a reassessment of Northern economic policies.

Stormont's economic policies had focused on meeting the needs of existing industry – unsurprising given that twelve out of Belfast's fourteen Stormont Members of Parliament (MPs) in the early 1950s were managing directors from established industry (Harbinson, 1973). Linen and shipbuilding were assisted through the Industrial Development Act, the Re-equipment of Industries Act and the Capital Grants to Industry Act. A 'coal subsidy' was created and, in 1959, de-rating for industry was retained at seventy-five per cent while in the British 'development areas' it was reduced to fifty per cent. This bias was challenged in the mid–1950s with the publication in 1957 of the 'Isles and Cuthbert' Report which argued that state assistance to existing industries was damaging the economy, and that only an influx of new capital to diversify the industrial base could raise industrial productivity. The report suggested that a 'Development Corporation' should be created to attract new multinational industries to the region and that industrial assistance should be re-orientated to meet their needs (Stormont, 1957).

However subsidisation continued and between 1955 and 1961, £123 million was spent on keeping existing firms afloat. In the same period, employment in textiles fell by 16,000 to 56,000, and in 1961, 8,000 workers were laid off from the shipyards, reducing the workforce to 16,000. In 1962, the government was again criticised for 'maintaining employment rather than creating jobs' and there was further confirmation of its failure since, between 1961 and 1964, another forty per cent of Belfast's shipyard workers were laid off (Stormont, 1962, p. 58; Bew, 1979, p. 134).

The economic proposals of the O'Neill government, outlined in the Wilson Report of 1964, were aimed at reversing this industrial decline. Paralleling the policies of the British Labour government, the proposals put great faith in planning for the 'expansion of industry, housing and public services'. This centralised planning framework led to a series of specific development plans. The Matthew Plan proposed the creation of eight 'growth centres', some of which were to be 'new towns' served by new or improved roads and by new public housing schemes. The Benson Plan proposed an improved rail system and the Lockwood Report outlined plans for a second Northern Ireland university. The result was a programme of state expenditure designed to improve social and economic infrastructure and to revitalise the local economy by attracting multinational capital to the region.

These measures mirrored Southern shifts in economic policy, themselves the outcome of a parallel economic crisis. Since 1932, de Valera's Fianna Fáil government had introduced a policy of economic autarchy aimed at increasing industrial growth through import substitution. High tariffs led to a forty per cent rise in industrial production from 1932 to 1936; industrial employment rose from 60,000 to 100,000 between 1926 and 1938, and continued to rise to 184,000 by 1951. But given limited domestic demand, this strategy had its limits, and by 1939 growth in industrial output had declined to single figures. Reflecting this, industrial employment began to fall after 1951 to 172,000 by 1960.

As in the North, this stimulated a shift in economic policy towards attracting international capital and towards export-orientated growth. Under pressure from the USA, and from the Organisation of European Economic Cooperation (OEEC), there had been some liberalisation of Irish trade during the short-lived Fine Gael governments of 1949–51 and 1954–57. There had also been some attempt at attracting overseas capital – in 1949 the Industrial Development Authority (IDA) was created (which only had limited powers until the Industrial Grants Act of 1956). Economic openness, however, only hastened the decline in industrial employment as increased trade liberalisation was coupled with a non-interventionist industrial policy and deflationary monetary policies.

It was only in the late 1950s that the Republic adopted a more expansionary, outward-looking economic policy. This led to a rapid convergence in economic orientation between the Republic and the North. The new Fianna Fáil government of 1959, with Sean Lemass as Minister for Trade and Commerce, introduced a range of measures (similar to those that were to be introduced in the early 1960s by the Northern O'Neill government) in order to attract international capital and to increase exports. The IDA's grant-giving activities were extended; from 1964 there were no controls on profit repatriation or on overseas ownership and control, and from 1958 a tax holiday on export revenue was introduced.

The Republic applied for membership of the General Agreement on Tariffs and Trade (GATT) in 1960 and of the EEC in 1961 (immediately after Britain). In 1963, it began reducing tariffs, culminating in the Anglo–Irish Free Trade Agreement of 1965. This had an immediate impact, with a doubling of the total volume of exports and imports from 1958 to 1972 (O'Brien, 1993). While competition for domestic markets led to some 30,000 job losses, increased sales by existing companies overseas, as well as increased international investment, created an estimated 75,000 jobs, leading to a significant overall net increase in industrial employment between 1960 and 1974 – to about 217,000 (Walsh, 1979).

In both parts of Ireland there was an attempt to 'hook on to' the post-war 'Fordist' wave of production, from which both had been excluded (Mjoset, 1993, p. 272). As the South moved away from economic autarchy and the North shifted from the single-minded support of existing declining industries, the two parts of Ireland began competing for international capital on a very similar development path. There was rapid convergence in economic orientations and employment structures as Ireland, North and South, gained a large multinational-controlled sector producing consumer goods for export.

Renewed North–South divergence

These pressures for convergence were short-circuited by sharpened political and military conflict in the North, resulting in renewed divergence from the early 1970s. As the conflict intensified, the Northern economy went into rapid decline and became increasingly dependent on British state subsidies; in contrast, the South sustained a thriving overseas sector and became increasingly dependent on overseas markets and multinational corporations.

In Northern Ireland, manufacturing employment 'suffered an astonishing' decline of some 20,000 jobs between 1971 and 1981 (Kennedy, 1988, p. 26). Industry shed forty per cent of its labour force due to on-going structural decline in shipbuilding and textiles, and also in the 'new' multinational sectors such as synthetic textiles. In place of these jobs, Northern Ireland attracted an increasing level of British Treasury funds, and the public sector grew from employing twenty-five per cent of the workforce in 1971 to thirty-eight per cent by 1983. Following the sharp depression of the early 1980s, Northern industry failed to participate in the economic recovery of the mid to late 1980s, and by the end of the decade a further 42,000 manufacturing jobs had been lost (Munck, 1993, p. 137). Unemployment had risen, seemingly permanently, from seven to fourteen per cent, meaning that by 1983, some fifty-two per cent of the North's working population was directly dependent on British state expenditure, while many more, up to a third, were indirectly dependent on its 'multiplier' effects.

A major factor in this was the dramatic decline in inward investment, which proved to be highly sensitive to phases of political conflict. Northern Ireland attracted about fifteen per cent of UK-bound Foreign Direct Investment between 1966 and 1970, falling to six per cent between 1970 and 1975. With relative political stability in the second half of the 1970s, inflows rose to ten per cent of the UK total, only to plummet virtually to zero during the period of intensified conflict in the early 1980s. There was a partial recovery during the short-lived UK economic recovery in the late 1980s, again coinciding with some diminution in the intensity of the conflict (Fothergill and Guy, 1990; O'Malley, 1985).[2]

Lacking continued capital inflows, overall employment went into decline. This was exacerbated by the oil crisis and recession from 1972, and intensified throughout the 1970s, culminating in widespread disinvestment as Sterling became overvalued from 1979 to 1983. In 1986, the proportion of manu-facturing jobs in externally owned firms stood at thirty-nine per cent, compared with fifty-three per cent in 1973, and remained at this level into the 1990s (Hamilton, 1993, p. 203). Between 1973 and 1986, multinational branch-plant closures cut Northern Ireland's industrial workforce by a quarter and by the mid 1980s, over half of the jobs that had been created by attracting overseas capital in the early 1960s, diversifying the North's industrial base into synthetic fibres, mechanical and electrical engineering, had disappeared. The resulting job losses, 36,000 between 1973 and 1986, have been cited as the main 'explanation' of the North's poor industrial performance in comparison with the Republic (Hamilton, 1993, p. 206).

This poor performance occurred despite government attempts to attract and retain overseas capital through the Industrial Development Board (IDB) (set up in 1976 as the Northern Ireland Development Agency), which spent £1 billion supporting industry in the 1980s. British government concern at the apparent failure of its economic policies led to a rethink in the 1987 *Pathfinder Process*, aimed at reducing Northern dependency on the British Treasury – perhaps an unrealistic goal given that the British subsidy accounted for thirty per cent of regional Gross Domestic Product (GDP). The 'path' chosen was one of stimulating increased local competitiveness and productivity, particularly through smaller-scale private sector 'enterprise' with minimal state interference, ignoring the impor-tance of the public sector in the North (Munck, 1993, p. 63). The subsequent policy document *Competing in the 1990s* similarly relied on ill-defined notions of competitiveness as the main criteria for IDB grant-giving, again neglecting the option of marshalling public sector finance and governance to redevelop the Northern economy (Clulow and Teague, 1993).

Instead of stimulating private sector manufacturing, gov-ernment spending boosted local services. Reflecting the growth in net public expenditure, from fourteen per cent of total domestic expenditure in 1970 to twenty-three per cent in 1979 and close to thirty per cent in 1993, there was substantial growth in retail and financial services which expanded to meet the needs of public sector employees. In 1974, distribution, hotels, catering and repairs accounted for nine per cent of total

21

regional GDP; by 1992 they accounted for twelve per cent. More spectacularly, finance, banking and real estate accounted for six per cent of GDP in 1974 and fifteen per cent in 1992. This contrasted with the manufacturing industry, which accounted for thirty-one per cent of GDP in 1974, falling to nineteen per cent by 1992.[3]

Despite deindustrialisation and substantial growth in the public sector, the Northern labour market remained highly sectarianised. As illustrated in Table 1.1, there was some increase in the proportion of Catholics employed in managerial and professional occupations. Catholics had become more represented in management, supervisory and professional roles, forming a new middle class heavily concentrated in the public sector (Cormack and Osborne, 1994). In 1991 for instance, Catholics accounted for forty-one per cent of teaching professionals and thirty-one per cent of health professionals but only twenty-two per cent of engineers and technologists.

This was offset by an increase in the Catholic population as a proportion of the total workforce, and a parallel, though not so rapid, increase in the proportion of unemployment accounted

Table 1.1 CATHOLICS IN THE NORTHERN IRELAND LABOUR MARKET

	1971	1991
Percentage of total economically active population	28.0	35.0
Percentage of unemployed		
– female	41.4	46.4
– male	47.0	52.4
Percentage of managers		
– large establishments	10.4	23.9
– small establishments	18.1	26.8
Percentage of supervisors		
– blue collar	20.7	30.2
– white collar	20.6	32.0
Percentage of professional employees	11.9	26.6
Percentage of self employed		
– without employees	25.6	33.4
– with employees	32.6	35.0

Source: 1971, 1991 Census, Central Statistics Office (CSO)

for by Catholics. There was only a slight decline in relative exclusion from employment: in 1971, Catholics accounted for twenty-eight per cent of the 'economically active' workforce and forty-seven per cent of Northern Ireland's male unemployed; by 1991, thirty-five per cent of the Northern Ireland workforce was Catholic and Catholic males comprised fifty-two per cent of total male unemployment. This translated into a widening unemployment differential between the two communities. As illustrated in Table 1.2, the differential between Catholic male unemployment and non-Catholic male unemployment widened from 9.7 per cent to 14.4 per cent, while for Catholic and non-Catholic women the differential widened from 3.1 per cent to 5.7 per cent.

This differential was compounded by sharpened income disparities. In the 1980s especially, Northern Ireland's middle class became significantly better off while the incomes of male unskilled or unemployed workers stagnated. The poorest ten per cent of the population earned on average £53 in 1979, rising in real terms to £56 in 1988, significantly lower than other regions in the UK. This compared with the richest ten per cent, whose weekly income increased to the same average level as the rest of the UK, at a rate of increase unmatched elsewhere (Ditch and Morrissey, 1992).

In general terms, with close to forty per cent of employees employed in the public sector at UK rates of pay, and with twenty per cent of Catholics and ten per cent of Protestants unemployed, the 'gap between the haves and the have-nots [was] very wide indeed' (Smyth, 1993, p. 138). On-going

Table 1.2 PERCENTAGE UNEMPLOYED IN NORTHERN IRELAND

	1971	1991
Catholic		
– females	6.9	14.5
– males	17.2	28.3
Non-Catholic		
– females	3.8	8.8
– males	7.5	13.9

Source: 1971, 1991 Census, CSO.

sectarian division, combined with sharpening income disparities in an economy dominated by a public sector, shaped economic interests in quite different ways from the Republic.

In contrast to Northern Ireland, the Republic's industrial policy was relatively successful into the late 1970s. The Republic's entry into the EU confirmed a rapid diversification of trading relations away from British markets and towards the continental EU. The rapid growth in Southern, mostly multinational, exports outweighed Irish–British trade, which in relative terms fell during the 1970s; a reorientation away from the British economy which was confirmed with the Republic's entry into the EU Exchange Rate Mechanism (ERM) in 1979 (New Ireland Forum (NIF) 1984a, p. 116).

Southern industry was dominated by multinational corporations. From employing twenty-seven per cent of the manufacturing workforce in 1973, the foreign owned sector employed forty-three per cent in 1986 and forty-five per cent by 1990. These firms were concentrated in relatively advanced industrial sectors – primarily in engineering and to a lesser extent in chemicals and synthetic clothing (Hamilton, 1993, p. 203). These foreign owned plants were largely de-linked from the local economy as tax breaks for exporters remained in place and plants were often located away from concentrations of domestically owned industry. Partly as a consequence, there was little indigenous development in the key sectors of auto, steel, electrical goods or durable consumer goods: Irish indigenous production in these sectors stood at fifteen per cent of industrial employment in 1978 while in the EU as a whole it stood at fifty-six per cent (Mjoset, 1993). Employment in foreign owned manufacturing grew by some twenty-two per cent in the period from 1973 to 1980 (to 80,000), while employment in indigenously owned sectors declined by some seven per cent over the same period (to 102,000), at least partly due to intensified competition in Irish domestic markets (National Economic and Social Council (NESC), 1983, pp. 299, 360). Reflecting the relative decline of indigenous industry, profit repatriation as a proportion of total industrial profits rose dramatically from fifteen per cent in 1975 to thirty per cent in 1980 and then to fifty per cent in the mid 1980s (Bradley et al., 1993). By the 1980s, multinationals accounted for over eighty per cent of all non-food exports, half of which were in electronics and chemicals; as the Organisation for Economic Cooperation and Development (OECD) put it in 1985, 'the Republic had become the "export platform" for multinational trade into the EEC' (OECD 1985, p. 47).

This pattern of EU-orientated dependent industrialisation was highlighted in the early 1980s as international recession sent domestically owned firms into rapid decline. A fall-off in foreign investment, higher capital intensity of incoming multinational plants, rapid deflation in UK markets and a fiscal squeeze in the Republic all contributed to an economic collapse which led to a twenty per cent reduction in manufacturing employment between 1982 and 1987. In the later 1980s, fiscal stability and a return to consensual corporatism (that had broken down in the late 1970s), combined with international growth to create a partial recovery. The *Programme for National Recovery* of 1987–90 constructed an explicit package of trade-offs between pay policy, welfare and taxation – although it failed to address the on-going problem of virtual tax exemption for exporting companies – both indigenous and multinational – and low rural taxation. Inward investment increased and manufacturing employment rose by some 15,000; but only 2,000 of the new jobs were based in indigenous industry and profit repatriation again increased as a proportion of total industrial profits, to sixty per cent by 1989 (O'Hearn, 1993). The balance of payments moved into surplus, Gross National Product (GNP) grew and unemployment fell, but by only four percentage points, from eighteen per cent in 1987 to fourteen per cent in 1990.

The Republic entered the 1990s with a manufacturing sector employing 19.2 per cent of the workforce – the same relative size as in 1973 (Bradley et al., 1993, OECD, 1991, p. 57). Growth in GDP lagged behind growth in exports so that by 1993, exports accounted for fifty-six per cent of GDP, in contrast with an EU average of twenty-two per cent (O'Donnell, 1993a, p. 25). Furthermore, with a decline in multinational employment as well as indigenous employment in the 1980s, this dependence condemned the Republic to high, and apparently permanent, levels of unemployment, at over fifteen per cent of the workforce.

Lacking a domestically owned industrial base, the Republic faced the prospect of maintaining high levels of inward investment to compensate for job losses as earlier waves of overseas capital relocated or simply closed down, reflecting wider shifts in global and EU production (Mjoset, 1993, p. 386). Government awareness of the lack of Irish owned industry was reflected in the Telesis Report of 1983, which argued that a 'successful indigenously owned industry is, in the long run, essential for a high income economy' (NESC, 1983, p. 185). The Report spoke of the need for an 'integrated indigenous Development Charter' and suggested that the government reduce the grants given to multinational firms and increase the proportion allocated to indigenous exporters from less than forty per cent to seventy-five per cent by 1990 (NESC, 1983, p. 36).

Ten years later, the failure to follow these policies and refocus industrial policy was highlighted in the Culliton Report (Dublin Stationery Office (DSO), 1992a). It drew remarkably similar conclusions to the Telesis Report, leading one optimistic observer to suggest that by the 1990s, there had emerged a 'widespread agreement that Ireland must develop competitive indigenous activity on a significantly larger scale if it is to meet its long-term income, social and employment aspirations' (O'Donnell, 1993a, p. 96). There were some indications that such concerns were translating into new public sector responses; the Republic's National Development Plan of 1994–99, for instance, envisaged spending approximately half of the total funds allocated for industrial assistance on locally-based employment strategies, focusing on the development of community infrastructure, to address the problem of long-term unemployment. Nonetheless, the remaining fifty per cent of industrial assistance – roughly the same proportion as in the early 1980s – was still to be spent on attracting and retaining multinational capital. Perhaps more important, such initiatives were overshadowed by the neo-classical, 'enterprise' –orientated *Programme for Competitiveness and Work*, 1994–97, which explicitly linked rates of growth of pay to inflation rates as the Republic sought to compete as a 'labour-intensive, low-cost, low-wage production centre' on the EU periphery (Hazelkorn and Patterson, 1994, p. 65).

Despite the relative success of neo-corporatist programmes in the South, in comparison with market orientated, 'enterprise' initiatives in the North, the economy remained unable to develop a viable indigenous sector. The policy of economic 'openness' – the removal of trade barriers, restrictions on foreign ownership of industry and financial regulations – continued to constrain economic policy (Bradley et al., 1993). Dominated by international capital and dependent on export markets, the Republic had great difficulty in developing the 'national system of innovation' that was required if the economy was to sustain an indigenous sector and stimulate 'autocentric' growth (Mjoset, 1993, p. 386).

Instead, the Republic more closely fitted into an 'extroverted' growth pattern – a pattern of economic growth without economic development (Amin, 1980). This is clearly illustrated by figures for the Republic's relative *per capita* GDP and its GNP. As a measure of total national income, GDP includes the repatriated profits of foreign owned companies and therefore overestimates income levels in the South. As illustrated in Table 1.3, there was a dramatic increase in net outflows of property income from 1980 to 1990, which was only partially offset by EU subsidies. As a result, GNP fell as a percentage of GDP, from 101 per cent in 1970 to eighty-eight per cent in 1990.

Table 1.3 GROSS GDP AND GNP: THE REPUBLIC OF IRELAND

(IR£, millions)	1970	1980	1990
GDP (market prices)	1,620	9,361	27,093
Net property income from abroad	+26	–392	–3,131
EU subsidies	zero	348	1,306
GNP (market prices)	1,648	9,002	23,961
GNP as a percentage of GDP	102	96	88

Source: National Accounts, aggregates, 1970–90 Eurostat, 1993; National Income and Expenditure, DSO, 1993.

Overall, the Republic fell 'into the twilight zone for both economic and political reasons' (Gillespie et al., 1992, p. 30). The economy was incipiently dualistic. In some respects, it was dramatically out-performing its economic partners while in others, it was seriously malfunctioning – reflected in the success of multinational companies in contrast with the decline of indigenous industry. Politically, as an enthusiastic EU member state, the Republic sought independence from the orbit of Britain, yet was tied to Britain, not only in its cultural and economic relations but also in its aspiration to unity with the North. These economic and political dualities which express tensions between a regional and a national development framework are further explored in Chapter Two.

In the two parts of Ireland, the 1970s and 1980s saw a marked divergence in patterns of development and dependency. The end of the post-War boom in Western Europe had disrupted the process of economic 'modernisation' in the two economies. With intensified conflict against a background of sharp economic recession, the North reverted to deepened deindustrialisation and to sharpened dependency on Britain; the South, for its part, sustained a programme of industrialisation with a temporary surge in transnational investment, becoming more dependent on non-British product markets and sources of capital.

By way of contrast, there was a potential return to convergence in the early 1990s. In both parts of Ireland, there was a partial rejection of the externally orientated strategy for economic development. In the North, the strategy had failed to reverse deindustrialisation after the upsurge in conflict from the early 1970s; in the South, it had failed to foster advanced, indigenously owned industry, especially in the face of sharpened economic recession in the 1980s. With British intimations that state subsidies would not always be available to prop up the Northern economy, and with Southern concerns at the collapse of indigenous employment and the fall-off in inward investment during the 1980s and 1990s, there was an increasing, common awareness of the necessity for policies aimed at generating indigenous 'systems of innovation' (DSO, 1992a, Mjoset, 1993). This shifting orientation in the latter years of the twentieth century, in the context of EU integration, is also discussed in Chapter Two.

1.2 POLITICAL CONFLICT

Economic divisions in Ireland are associated with a variety of ideological and political divisions, principally between Irish nationalists and British or Ulster unionists. As has been mentioned, these were a major factor, along with British state policy, in the Partition of the island into two separate jurisdictions in 1921. In the late 1960s and early 1970s, nationalist–unionist conflicts refocused on Northern Ireland, and became a central factor in renewed North–South divergence.

Unionism and Loyalism

In Northern Ireland, the Ulster Unionist Party (UUP) exercised power in the newly partitioned statelet. The political alliance between working-class Loyalism and middle-class (and landed) Unionism, expressed in the UUP, rested on ties of patronage which were disrupted by industrial decline and by the attempts at 'modernising' Northern industry. In the mid 1960s industrialists and their employees in the declining sectors, and local government officials, came out in firm opposition to the liberal Unionist would-be 'modernisers', leading to intense political conflict within the Unionist Party. As the collapse of Northern industry dissolved the mechanics of patronage, the working-class allies of élite Unionism took to the streets with increasingly insistent assertions of Protestant ascendancy, that significantly 'took place in the absence of visible nationalist irredentism' (O'Leary and Arthur, 1990, p. 35).

This breakdown in UUP hegemony can be understood in economic terms. Some have argued, for instance, that the non-sectarian employment practices of foreign owned firms, closing the divide between the 'skilled' Protestant and the 'unskilled' Catholic labour force, was a major factor (Probert, 1978). But both the (assumed) non-sectarian employment practices of multinational companies and the deskilling of the workforce had little impact on Protestant privilege as the growth areas, announced under the modernisers' employment expansion plans, were largely located in Protestant districts (the 'Matthew' plan). Indeed, there is more evidence that the attempts at restructuring industry accommodated rather than challenged sectarian divisions. For instance, ninety per cent of the new job vacancies were filled privately rather than via the employment exchange, and Catholic unemployment remained substantially higher than Protestant unemployment (O'Dowd, 1980a, 1980b; Bew et al., 1979, p. 189). The explosion of Protestant extremism in declining urban communities, like the Shankill and Woodvale, came when economic recovery had begun to increase employment opportunities for this class of workers. A more likely explanation then, is that assertions of working-class loyalism emerged as a response to the feared – rather than actual – consequences of dismantling Northern industry, in terms of its implications for unionist hegemony as well as for the privileged position of some skilled Protestant workers. This interpretation accords a key role to political factors in generating conflict, as opposed to economic interests.

Changing economic circumstances forced Protestant workers away from the UUP as it was no longer seen as serving their interests. Initially their dissent was expressed through the Northern Irish Labour Party (NILP) that from 1949 had become pro-Partition. Throughout the 1950s, the NILP acted as a 'loyal' opposition in Stormont, campaigning against the Unionist government on social issues, and when redundancies in declining industries started to accelerate in the late 1950s, the party was the natural beneficiary of working-class Protestant dissent. Protestant workers in constituencies such as Woodvale and Victoria voted four NILP members into Stormont in 1958 (all four were Protestant lay preachers), and in 1962, after further redundancies, the NILP vote rose by fifteen per cent.

From 1961, however, the NILP had to compete with working-class 'Unionist Associations' that championed the right of 'loyal' (i.e. Protestant) workers to preferential employment in Northern Irish industry. Linking their politics to the defence of the 'Union', these associations were unapologetic in their determination to extend Protestant ascendancy, and were fully capable of taking their politics onto the streets. Protestant leaders like Ian Paisley and the unionist MP for Shankill, Desmond Boal, worked within the 'Committee for the Defence of the Constitution' to pressurise the Unionist government into addressing the demands of Protestant workers. While Paisley campaigned for continued preferential allocation of

Council housing to Protestant tenants, Boal campaigned for the Prime Minister, Lord Brookeborough, to honour commitments to Protestant workers. Partly as a result, in 1963 Brookeborough was replaced by O'Neill, who was soon challenged by the Committee to demonstrate his commitment to Protestant ascendancy. In 1964, for instance, when the Committee called for the Royal Ulster Constabulary (RUC) to remove a tricolour displayed in the window of a Nationalist Party campaign headquarters in West Belfast, O'Neill hesitated, and a series of demonstrations were staged, leading to the worst rioting Belfast had seen since 1935. Recognising the necessity to retain the support of disaffected Protestant workers, O'Neill bowed to pressure from the Committee and ordered the RUC to remove the tricolour.

By 1964 the NILP had lost two of its four seats in Stormont – one to the Protestant Workers Association in Woodvale. Dissent was also expressed through the politics of violent sectarianism, most clearly through the Ulster Volunteer Force (UVF) which was revived 'to execute known IRA men', and who shot four Catholics in three separate incidents in May 1966. Throughout the summer of that year, Catholic houses in Protestant districts were petrol-bombed by Loyalist youths, and by 1969, after three summers of sectarian riot, Paisley's 'Protestant Unionist Party' (PUP) was drawing Protestant voters away from the UUP. In West Ulster (Derry), the PUP gained 20,000 votes, and after O'Neill resigned from Stormont, Paisley was voted in as the MP for Bannside. In 1970, Paisley gained a Westminster seat in North Antrim. Boal left the Unionist Party to join him and, in 1971, the party was renamed the 'Democratic Unionist Party' (DUP). By the early 1980s, it was gaining a twenty per cent share of the votes cast in Northern Ireland and Paisley's brand of unionism had established itself as the most vocal expression of Protestant disaffection in the North.

The emergence of the DUP signalled a split in the loyalist–unionist alliance, and was a major factor in the dissolution of Stormont and the imposition of Direct Rule from Westminster in 1972. Ironically, the DUP later argued that the conflict would only be resolved if Northern Ireland returned to a majority-dominated Assembly on the Stormont model. In contrast, the UUP argued that the national conflict would only be solved when Northern Ireland was fully part of the British state. The anomalous status of Northern Ireland – ruled by the Westminster Parliament but not fully integrated with Britain – was seen as an encouragement to those pushing for a reunited Ireland. So too was the implication in British constitutional legislation that Northern Ireland need only remain part of the United Kingdom so long as a majority in Northern Ireland wished it (Coughlan, 1992). This UUP 'integrationist' agenda was particularly associated with James Molyneaux, and formerly Enoch Powell, although, in the face of pressure from the 'devolutionist' strand of unionism during the 1980s, 'integrationists' began to accept the possibility of 'decentralisation', provided there were similar provisions for Wales and Scotland. This adaptation of the 'integrationist' approach, as reiterated by Molyneaux in May 1992, maintained the essential argument that only the full exercise of British sovereignty would resolve the conflict.[4]

The UUP and the 'liberal unionist' Alliance Party remained largely representative of the 'Ulster British' wing of unionism which emphasised its cultural links with Britain but was also willing to see itself, in some respects, as Irish. This contrasted with the DUP and other loyalist organisations, such as the Ulster Defence Association (UDA), which were actively hostile to the South and expressed a more 'Ulster loyalist' political identity, whose primary loyalty was to the Northern Ireland political order rather than to Britain (Todd, 1987). The paramilitary UDA pushed this latter position to its logical extreme in arguing that both the British and the Irish states should forgo their claims to sovereignty over the North and allow the creation of an independent sovereign Northern Ireland.

Despite these differences, Unionist and Loyalist politicians remained unified on the single central issue of opposition to Irish unity. They often worked together against nationalism, most notably in 1974 when the British government capitulated to a loyalist–unionist alliance that included the Ulster Workers' Committee, the United Army Council of the UDA/UVF, the DUP and the UUP, which had orchestrated a fourteen-day stoppage against the Anglo–Irish Sunningdale Agreement (Millar, 1978; Fisk, 1975). Similar alliances, in 1979 against the

Constitutional Convention and in 1986 against the Anglo–Irish Agreement (AIA), were less successful, with the AIA being left to 'wither on the vine' as Jim Molyneaux leader of the UUP put it, rather than being directly brought down by unionist action.

In the 1990s then, unionist politics was dominated by two main parties – the Unionist Party claiming approximately thirty per cent of the Northern vote and the DUP claiming about twenty per cent. A third party, the Alliance Party, which also emerged in the early 1970s to inherit the 'liberal' modernising strand of unionism, claimed about eight per cent of the Northern vote. Political dispute between the three parties centred on the degree of hostility to the South, defined in terms of their willingness to accept power-sharing with the nationalist community and to tolerate North–South linkages. Changing unionist positions on this last issue are discussed in some detail in Chapter Three.

Nationalism and Republicanism

Partition led to North–South divergence between a Northern nationalist community still committed to North–South unity and an increasingly stable and 'completed' nationalist community in the South. Since 1922, Northern nationalists had 'watched their fellow Irish nationalists abandon them bit by bit'.[5] While for the Northern parties, North-South unity was a central issue, for the southern-based parties, it was only of primary concern when political violence threatened to spread southwards.

This reflected the origins of Irish nationalism as a movement primarily concerned with power relationships between Ireland and Britain, rather than between North and South in Ireland. Ideological conflict over the Republic's relationship with Britain shaped political forces in the post-independence period; the Southern two-party political system developed out of the civil war and focused on the pro-Treaty (Fine Gael) and anti-Treaty (Fianna Fáil) factions of the Irish nationalist movement. With the 1937 Constitution, the political boundaries of the Irish nationalist project had, for the most part, been defined. Although there remained a question mark over Northern

Ireland, expressed in Articles Two and Three of the Constitution, this was a largely peripheral concern to the main project of establishing an Irish political culture free of British domination. As a result, there was considerable consensus between the two main wings of the Republic's political system – a consensus that was silent on issues of North–South unity and equally important, prevented significant political, left–right, capital–labour conflict.

Indeed, the incorporation of a Protestant-dominated Northern Ireland into the Republic was never a desirable objective for those who gained from the creation of an autarchic, 'national' economy and a conservative 'national' society. Rural, export-orientated commerce, and those that depended on it, had backed the Fine Gael Party that took power in the immediate post-Partition period. Successive Fine Gael governments attempted to liberalise the Southern economy, and in the 1980s, under Garret Fitzgerald, the party made some attempt at relaxing some of the more restrictive aspects of Irish social legislation, for instance, in the unsuccessful referenda on decriminalising reproductive rights (1983) and divorce (1986). On the national question, the party was committed to substantial revision of the Irish constitutional claim to sovereignty in the North and it maintained a largely anti-Republican perspective, arguing for North–South unity on the basis of shared sovereignty in the EU – a 'non-magical, lawyers', pragmatic nationalism'.[6]

Meanwhile, the more populist Fianna Fáil Party that emerged in 1932, drew support from farmers, traders and workers dependent upon domestic markets and, under de Valera, dominated Irish politics during the 1940s and 1950s. The party attempted to mould mass national unity – a 'vision of the Republic as a moral community' – with it as the 'natural' party of government.[7] This was pursued first, through national autarchy and, from 1958 under Sean Lemass, through state intervention and economic liberalisation, a model that shaped its policies into the 1990s. The party combined a broadly pro-unification perspective with this consensual vision of Southern society, and it was more willing than Fine Gael to support the Republic's constitutional claim to jurisdiction in the North, although in government it did little to make it a reality.

There was a clear divergence in constitutional nationalism between these southern-based Fine Gael and Fianna Fáil parties, and the northern Nationalist Party, which became the Social Democratic and Labour Party (SDLP) in 1971. This was also, to a great extent, true of the Republican movement which split in 1969 into a Northern-based 'Provisional' IRA (PIRA) and the 'Officials', which later formed the Workers' Party (which itself split in 1992 with the formation of the southern-based Democratic Left).

Increasingly however, from the 1970s, political conflict along a range of new political issues began to penetrate political life in the Republic and began to disrupt the two main political blocs. The Fine Gael – Fianna Fáil divide between bourgeois nationalism and populist nationalism was increasingly cross-cut and undermined by a multitude of new political divisions. These focused on neo-liberal versus social democratic issues, and on issues of gender and the family, sexuality and religion – issues that had previously been kept off the political agenda by the nationalist consensus dating back to 1937.

In the 1980s, under Charles Haughey's leadership, the more anti-nationalist and neo-liberal right wing of the Fianna Fáil Party departed to form the Progressive Democrats. After the 1989 election, this forced Fianna Fáil into a parliamentary coalition for the first time in its history, forcing it to discard its pretension to express the 'national' political will 'above' party politics. Partly as a result of these and other political pressures, the candidate supported by Fianna Fáil was defeated in the 1990 presidential election and Mary Robinson, the candidate supported by Labour, was voted in. In 1992, the Irish Labour Party was able to double its popular vote to nineteen per cent and increase its representation in the Dáil from sixteen to thirty-three, at the expense of Fine Gael and Fianna Fáil, in an election that also saw the Progressive Democrats increase their representation by four seats.[8] Furthermore, in the European election of 1994, the Irish Green Party gained two seats in the European Parliament (EP) and the Democratic Left had a by-election victory, in a further disruption of political relations.

In parallel with this destabilisation of Southern politics, there was an increased orientation towards Northern concerns. This largely reflected the intensifying political and military conflict in the North. In the mid 1960s, Protestant extremism reemerged at a time when Nationalists and Republicans had been reconciling themselves to Northern politics. The IRA effectively abandoned the armed struggle after the failed 'Border Campaign' of 1959, and in 1965 the Northern Nationalist Party ended abstentionism and entered Stormont as the 'official' opposition. Heightened cross-community political mobilisation on social and political issues through the civil rights movement (with the 'Campaign for Social Justice' of 1964, the 'Campaign for Democracy in Ulster' in 1966, the 'Northern Ireland Civil Rights Association' in 1967 and 'People's Democracy' in 1968) destabilised the Northern government's attempts at economic 'modernisation' and highlighted the political and social exclusion of the Northern nationalist minority. There was an upsurge in police violence against the Northern nationalist community, in particular the RUC attack on Derry's Bogside in February 1969, followed by a wave of sectarian attacks against Belfast Catholics in the summer of 1969, which forced 1,505 Catholic households to leave the city (a significant proportion of its 28,616 Catholic households).

As Catholic refugees began arriving in Dublin, Southern nationalist politicians were forced to reverse their inward-looking political strategy. Politicians from the Republic worked with constitutional nationalists in the North, represented in the newly emergent SDLP. They encouraged the British government to construct North–South political institutions, reflected in the Anglo–Irish Sunningdale Agreement of 1973, which was later broken by the British government, under loyalist–unionist pressure. Despite this initial failure, the new political conditions were forcing nationalist political parties, North and South, to reformulate their central demand for Irish unity (Coughlan, 1990). Proposals tended to converge on the possibility of establishing all-Ireland, quasi-federal structures: in 1972, both the SDLP's *Towards a New Ireland* and the Provisional IRA's *New Ireland* programmes proposed a degree of autonomy for the North within a reunified Ireland. In the same year, Garret Fitzgerald's book, also titled *Towards a New Ireland*, took a similar approach, and in 1979 Fine Gael formally adopted federalism in its policy paper – *Ireland: Our Future Together*.

The Republican movement forced the pace of this North–
South reorientation with the IRA's decision in 1981 to relaunch
Sinn Féin as an all-Ireland political organisation, on a wave of
campaigns focused on the treatment of Republican prisoners in
British jails. This led to the reemergence of a radical, populist
movement dedicated to Irish national liberation as an alternative
to the SDLP's constitutional nationalism. Within two years, Sinn
Féin was drawing close to forty per cent of the Northern
Nationalist vote, directly threatening the survival of the SDLP.
In response, constitutional nationalists (SDLP, Fine Gael and
Fianna Fáil) established the New Ireland Forum (NIF) as a
means of reclaiming their right to speak for the Irish national
community. As a result, for the first time since Partition, constitutional nationalists, North and South, were unified behind a
common, constitutional agenda for Irish national reconciliation
and reunification, albeit as an alternative to the Republican
agenda pursued by Sinn Féin.

The NIF demonstrated that nationalists and republicans in
both parts of Ireland had focused on the issue of North–South
structures as a means of guaranteeing the rights of nationalist
communities in the North. This was expressed in the range of
schemes for achieving North–South accommodation:

- devolution for Ulster and possibly also the other three
  provinces in a reunified Irish state favoured for some time
  by de Valera and, until 1981, by the PIRA;
- a federal Ireland cantonised into thirty-two counties as
  proposed by Sean MacBride at the NIF;
- a federation or confederation of two units, North and
  South, which has been Fine Gael policy since 1979 and was
  presented by Garret Fitzgerald and by the SDLP at the NIF;
- the option of consociationalism involving the recognition of
  a distinct unionist identity, the construction of power-sharing
  arrangements in Northern Ireland and the abandonment of
  the Irish Nationalist objective to create an all-Ireland state,
  favoured by liberal unionists and 'revisionist' nationalists;
- and finally, the option of unified independent statehood,
  which was presented as the NIF's favoured option (New
  Ireland Forum, 1984b).

For the British government this refocusing of constitutional
nationalism, North and South, helped to put North–South

institutions back on the political agenda in Northern Ireland. Experiments with internal Northern Ireland structures, (the Constitutional Convention of 1979 and the Northern Ireland Assembly of 1982–6) had failed in the face of nationalist opposition. North–South structures offered the attractive possibility of recruiting the Southern state, and the Northern SDLP, as partners in maintaining Northern Ireland stability. This was reflected in intensified Anglo–Irish cooperation, which culminated in the Anglo–Irish Agreement (AIA) of 1985 and created permanent and formal intergovernmental institutions, with the promise of North–South institutions should Northern Unionists fail to agree on power-sharing devolution.

By the late 1980s, following the NIF and the AIA, the three main southern parties – Fianna Fáil, Fine Gael and the Labour Party – had accepted what was effectively SDLP leadership on North–South issues. The SDLP stress on the need for a North–South 'dimension' to Irish politics, expressed in its support for the Sunningdale Agreement, was strengthened in the 1980s with an increased commitment to the process of European integration. The party linked EU integration to national integration in Ireland, arguing for a redefinition of Irish and British state sovereignty alongside a wholesale transformation of civil authority in the new EU framework. In its view, the nation state was being eroded 'from above' by transnational EU structures, and undermined 'from below' by sub-state regional pressures – a dual development that would remove the main basis of the national conflict in Ireland.

Meanwhile, in the face of political deadlock, Sinn Féin was also redefining its political position. In the late 1980s, the party began to move away from arguing that all-Ireland sovereignty was a non-negotiable, absolute requirement for peace in Ireland. Its position was increasingly recast as a positive-sum aspiration to unitary sovereignty in which there was recognition of the numerous obstacles, in particular of the need to accommodate Northern unionism, in social, cultural, economic and security terms. This position was outlined in its policy document, *Toward a Lasting Peace*, published in 1992, which signalled a shift away from the all-or-nothing discourse of military conflict to the more compromising discourse of democratic politics. The shift, when accompanied by PIRA and UDA/UVF ceasefires in the summer of 1994, began a 'peace process' that for the first time linked republicanism and constitutional nationalism, which was expressed through debates at the 'Forum for Peace and Reconciliation' set up by the Dublin government in October 1994.

This had the effect of shifting the political agenda away from issues relating to the military conflict – issues that had dominated political debates in the Republic. While Southern popular aspiration to unity was increasing (see Chapter Three), there was widespread war-weariness and a tendency towards an emotional rejection of Northern nationalist concerns. This political and emotional distance was highlighted in March 1993 when the Irish Head of State, Mary Robinson, offered her official condolences to the families of the dead and injured after the IRA bombing in Warrington, only the second time that a Head of State had publicly voiced concern at killings related to the conflict (the last time had been after the Bloody Sunday killings, twenty years previously). The bombing stimulated a wave of peace demonstrations in Dublin marked with 'bitter irony' when the parents of children killed by plastic bullets in the North were refused the right to speak at demonstrations outside the General Post Office (GPO) in the centre of Dublin.[9] The PIRA ceasefire removed this barrier to Southern involvement, allowing the clearer articulation of political aspirations, and refocusing the political agenda on the key question of North–South political structures.

Overall, from the 1970s, North–South political conflict had to a large degree focused on issues of North–South integration. Despite political divisions within the Northern unionist community, expressed in the emergence of the DUP and the Alliance, politicians from all three unionist parties competed for political support in the North within a broad consensus on the need to defend the Union and oppose North–South unity. Similarly, despite political differences, a degree of common purpose between republicans and nationalists, North and South, was maintained and indeed rebuilt – first with the NIF bringing constitutional nationalists together and second with the 1994–6 'peace process', bringing nationalists and republicans together. In the context of European integration, there were some indications that this process of reconciliation and political convergence was extending to the unionist parties. These, and other EU-related pressures are discussed in Chapter three.

After Partition, uneven development between North and South and ideological conflict between unionism and nationalism were exacerbated by divergent state policies. From 1921, state building, North and South, took place at the expense of pan-Irish nation building as the island was partitioned into a Northern segment with a Protestant majority – from its inception an exercise in 'domination' – and a Southern state, linked to Britain through the Commonwealth and later fully independent (O'Leary and Arthur, 1990 p. 35; O'Leary and McGarry, 1990, p. 272). Northern Ireland was given a 'quasi federal' status within the UK, conditional on continued support for the 'Union', while the Republic defined itself as a separate sovereign state (Jay, 1989). Constitutional division underscored socio-economic and ideological divisions, allowing separate North–South development, along with a sharpening division between 'loyal' unionists and 'disloyal' nationalists in Northern Ireland.

In the North, political control was handed over to a Unionist Party that was the political manifestation of Protestant ascendancy. Throughout its existence, Stormont was dominated by the UUP – a party led by 'Orangemen'. Of the 149 Unionist MPs who sat in Stormont between 1921 and 1971, 135 were members of the Orange Order (Rumpf and Hepburn, 1977, p. 178). These MPs were largely free of UK Parliamentary interference – even in 1935, the year of the worst riots in Belfast since 1921, the UK Parliament spent one hour and thirty-five minutes discussing Northern Ireland.

Manipulation of elections maintained UUP control of the political system: in 1921, constituency boundaries were redrawn and the political system was gerrymandered so that by 1922 there were only two non-Unionist MPs and ten non-Unionist controlled Councils. In local elections, twenty-five per cent of the electorate was excluded as voting was conditional upon property ownership (three quarters of this property-less population were Catholics). In Stormont elections, the UUP introduced the 'first past the post' system in 1929 to present voters with a clear choice between nationalist and unionist candidates. All elections in Northern Ireland became 'sectarian elections' (as Beattie, NILP MP for East Belfast said in 1927), in which the odds were stacked against nationalist candidates: as a result, between 1929 and 1969 only forty per cent of elections were contested and local councils became dominated by UUP representatives. Meanwhile, a 'loyalty to the crown' oath effectively excluded nationalists from the Northern Ireland Civil Service and local government departments. This had a direct effect on access to public services: in the 1930s, for instance, Catholic families were systematically denied poor law relief, and during the house-building programmes of the 1950s and 60s, public housing was allocated in the first instance to the Protestant community.

There was some promise that the 1960s 'modernisation' programmes would bring an end to discrimination. The 1964 Wilson Report, for instance, led to the creation of a 'Housing Trust' with authority over local housing, and a centralised 'Ministry of Development' which removed key powers over transport, health and planning from local government, the main source of discriminatory provision (Stormont, 1964, p. 133–40). But the new bodies were created to shore up the Unionist bloc, not to challenge it; the political will to implement the Wilson plan had been born out of a UUP backbench revolt against Brookeborough amongst Unionists who were seeing the bedrock of working-class unionism slipping away from them. Not surprisingly then, of the eight new 'growth centres', only one was in a Catholic district (in Downpatrick); most of the new housing was built around these centres, and most of the employment was allocated to locals who were predominantly Protestant. The £35 million road-building programme designed to serve the growth centres was also focused in eastern, largely Protestant districts which already had a relatively well developed road network. Again, the new railways did not service major Catholic towns like Newry, and most controversial of all, the new university was to be sited on the Northern coast in the small Protestant town of Coleraine rather than in Northern Ireland's second largest city – Derry (Farrell, 1976).

Despite these efforts, Protestant working-class dissatisfaction with the UUP continued unabated and was paired with active opposition amongst the local administrative élite that had been robbed of their sources of power and patronage (O'Dowd, 1980a, p. 42). The threat to local administrative hegemony was compounded by the threat to vested interests in declining sectors of industry. Despite a persistent campaign waged by employers in the linen and shipbuilding industry, Stormont refused to introduce an employment subsidy and instead introduced grants for firms creating jobs and spent large sums of public money on improving infrastructure for the influx of new capital.

These sections of the unionist élite and the 'plebeian grass roots' of the Protestant class alliance retained a 'veto over what slight tendency the bourgeois leadership had to make pragmatic concessions' to the increasingly assertive civil rights movement (Farrell, 1983, p. 288). The O'Neill government was reduced to making 'symbolic gestures' of reconciliation with the South, for instance, meeting the Taoiseach, Sean Lemass, in 1964 and persuading the Nationalist Party to join Stormont in 1965 (Bew, 1979, p. 13). But he could not refuse Paisley's demands in 1964; nor could he do anything more than condemn the UVF for its 'strategy of tension' after it had declared that 'known IRA men will be executed' in 1966.

Under pressure from the civil rights movement, O'Neill introduced a new system of housing allocation on the basis of need, reviewed the Special Powers Act and established a new Derry Corporation. But he failed to accept the movements' central demands – for universal suffrage in local elections, a redrawing of election boundaries and a review of the RUC – demands that struck at the heart of Unionist–Orange hegemony. O'Neill's impotence was underlined in February 1969 when he failed to criticise the RUC attack on Derry's Bogside or halt anti-Catholic pogroms. Despite this, the UUP lost working-class support and, after the UVF bomb attacks in April 1969, O'Neill resigned in a move that presaged the collapse of Stormont and Direct Rule from Westminster in 1972.

The Southern state, meanwhile, had retained a studied ambivalence towards the North. As has been mentioned, from 1937, the Republic claimed jurisdiction over the North under Articles two and three of its Constitution. Despite this, and in contrast with often strident party rhetoric, the Irish state was only in a limited sense committed to substantive North–South integration. Instead, it tended to adopt a largely reactive, 'hands off' approach on such issues – as the former Taoiseach, Garret Fitzgerald, stressed in 1993, the Irish state was more concerned to maintain order and stability in the twenty-six counties than to remove British sovereignty in Northern Ireland.[10]

Southern politicians generally focused on the relationship with Britain rather than on North–South relationships. The North–South Council set up under the 1921 Government of Ireland Act, for instance, was viewed with some hostility as it was seen as linking the Southern state to Britain and involving implicit recognition of the Northern statelet. The South also maintained its distance due to the jurisdictional logic of Partition as, from 1921, Southern politicians were elected by voters in the twenty-six Counties and were primarily responsible to them, not to voters in the North. Consequently, whenever Southern state priorities conflicted with North–South unity, the former generally prevailed.

Even the anti-Treaty Fianna Fáil Party, first elected in 1932, was relatively unconcerned with the North. De Valera's government was more preoccupied in political conflicts with Britain (for instance over land annuities and the use of ports) leading it, for the most part, to ignore North–South relations. The Constitution, agreed by referendum in 1937, focused on the issue of leaving the Commonwealth, ceasing the oath of allegiance to the British monarch and removing the British Governor-General from Dublin. While it laid claim to jurisdiction in the North, there was little attempt to exercise this; on the contrary, the Constitution had quite the opposite effect, as it established a 'special' role for the Catholic Church and cemented North–South, unionist–nationalist religious divisions. Southern politicians were engaged in constructing a 'national' – and Catholic – Irish culture against a history of British domination rather than building the conditions for unity.

This 'national' project enabled the two main political parties, Fine Gael and Fianna Fáil, to insulate themselves from the difficult cultural and religious questions raised by the requirement to work for North–South Irish unity. It also allowed the Republic's first President, Fianna Fáil's de Valera, to construct a highly centralised, corporatist administrative apparatus, expressing the myth of national unity. The Constitution explicitly relegated women to domestic roles, while the administrative structures relegated elected political representatives to the fringes of state-centred, consensus-forming institutions. The result was a political system that obscured or buried internal social cleavages in the name of national independence, partly at the cost of sharpening North–South cleavages.

Civil rights agitation in the North and the collapse of Stormont undermined this insulation, and from 1969, the Republic sought to persuade Britain to grant it a role in Northern administration. While initial concerns at sectarian violence were rebuffed by the British Labour government in 1969, Southern politicians were later granted a limited role through the Sunningdale Agreement. This was sustained through the Anglo–Irish intergovernmental consultation process from 1977 to 1985, and by the AIA of 1985. As the Southern state became more involved in Northern issues, some argued that the Republic could take the initiative and 'work the Anglo–Irish accord', to achieve greater North–South integration.[11] During 1994, this agenda was pursued to a limited extent by the Foreign Minister, Dick Spring, and the Taoiseach, Albert Reynolds, building on the Anglo–Irish Declaration of 1993, and explicitly involving the Republic, with the North and Britain, in the negotiating framework for 'national reconciliation' in the island as a whole.

Despite these political involvements, there was only limited substantive reorientation of socio-economic policies in the Republic and it remained firmly committed to development in separation from the North, rather than in tandem with it. Economic policy was increasingly orientated towards continental EU states, demonstrated for instance by the decision to join the ERM in 1979. Social policy remained highly restrictive: the referenda on decriminalisation of abortion (1983) and legalisation of divorce (1986) both failed and a special role was preserved for religious organisations as providers of social services and education. The 1990s saw a limited shift towards a more inclusive approach with, for instance, the introduction of abortion in life-threatening circumstances, provision for divorce, again under strict conditions, and similar, very limited restrictions on the role of religious orders in the delivery of state services. The ensuing political struggles have convulsed the Republic, forcing it away from the settled identities, national and otherwise, expressed in the 1937 Constitution. These political conflicts challenge the sectarian categorisations that are the legacy of colonialism and Partition, and thereby open up the potential for firmer North–South linkages: as the *Irish Times* pointed out in relation to disputes over the provision of education – 'battles to be fought over our schools are also battles about the nation'.[12] The outcome of these battles hinges not only on Southern state action, but also on action in the North.

Direct Rule and North–South relations

Since 1972, Northern Ireland has been dominated by British state policies. Unlike the UUP-controlled Stormont, the British state cast itself in the role of neutral arbiter between nationalist and unionist aspirations in the North (sketched out in the government White Paper on Northern Ireland in 1972).[13] This was directly contradicted by its constitutional commitment to maintaining British sovereignty in the North as long as the Northern unionist majority desired it.

The Sunningdale Agreement of 1973 clearly expressed these tensions. The North–South Council set up under the Agreement was composed of an equal number of Northern and Southern representatives with a British appointed official, effectively an 'arbiter', to oversee the sharing of British power with the Republic. Revealingly, the entire Council framework was subject to the authority of the British Secretary of State, including the power to appoint members of the executive. Furthermore, key 'sovereign' powers involving the central issues in the Northern Ireland conflict – electoral arrangements, security, policing and justice – were all to be reserved for the British government.

This approach to Direct Rule was also reflected in political and administrative structures as the government made a concerted attempt to depoliticise the machinery of Northern Ireland government, transforming it into a technocracy of state officials headed by an English Secretary of State. Direct Rule was managed through ostensibly non-political officials of the Northern Ireland Civil Service, acting in concert through 'Political Co-ordination' committees; the role of local government was heavily circumscribed and finances were distributed through appointed boards such as the Police Authority (wholly appointed), Education Area Boards (forty per cent councillors), Health and Social Services Boards (no councillors) and the Northern Ireland Housing Executive (NIHE) (thirty per cent councillors) (Connolly, 1992). It was intended that this administrative apparatus and its array of semi-autonomous agencies would promote social and political equity between nationalists and unionists, integrating the nationalist minority as part of an inclusive Northern Ireland identity and thereby providing a common basis for British citizenship in Northern Ireland.

But, unavoidably, this inclusiveness was more often contradicted by exclusive definitions of Britishness. British state power in Northern Ireland was, in the last resort, designed 'to incorporate the population and underpin the Union' (Ditch and Morrissey, 1992). State initiatives were inevitably shaped by the logic of maintaining political stability and state hegemony; this meant maintaining unionist support, leaving sectarian labour relations in place and minimising North–South integration. At the same time, the British state had its own priorities, especially in relation to policing the republican community, which sharply conflicted with the process of building inclusive political institutions in the North. As a result, Direct Rule was unable to supersede the economic, cultural and political causes of the conflict, largely as they emanated from the structural logic of the British state itself (Ruane and Todd, 1991).

As part of the process of desectarianising Northern Ireland society, in 1976 the government established a 'Fair Employment Agency' (FEA) to stamp out Catholic disadvantage in the labour market. The Agency's 'Declaration of Principles' on fair employment were condemned by the Unionist Council in 1977 and were largely ignored until 1981 when local government contractors were forced to adopt the Declaration. By 1987, 6,335 firms had signed the Declaration, rising from twenty-four in 1981. Not one of these firms was found to have infringed FEA provisions, partly because the Agency could not require them to supply employment figures broken down into Protestant and Catholic until 1989. It was only in 1990, under the Fair Employment Act, that employers were encouraged to work towards fair employment, on pain of losing government contracts.

These weaknesses reflected the government's priorities. Indeed, in so far as it was directly involved in maintaining security in Northern Ireland, the British state was directly involved in maintaining sectarianism in the Northern labour market. Nationalists continued to be excluded from employment as they were seen by unionists and by the British government as, by definition, 'disloyal'. Falling Catholic employment in the security forces for instance, was not seen as discrimination, but as a logical consequence of nationalist antipathy to the Northern state and of the republican security threat. This was reflected in government policy, outlined in the 1976 Commons Statement establishing the FEA, where it was clarified that the prohibition of discrimination on grounds of political belief would not extend to those whose opinion would lead them to the 'approval or acceptance of the use of violence for political ends'.[14] Unionist politicians and employers adapted this to include all those who might conceivably support republican aims – in effect all Catholics – an interpretation that was legitimised by the Secretary of State in 1988 when the FEA was banned from investigating the exclusion of Catholic contract workers from the Kilroot power station.[15]

In other fields of social policy, such as housing, the picture was no less bleak. Like the FEA, the NIHE was granted wide-ranging powers to allocate housing on the basis of need and to manage housing estates in the interests of all tenants. While the executive was effective in moving Catholics away from Protestants and vice versa, it signally failed to pursue the perpetrators of sectarian violence and criminal damage. In April of 1986, for instance, during unionist protests against the AIA, there were 337 complaints of harassment or assault and seventy-nine arson attacks, followed by a further 114 in July of the same year. Many Catholic householders were moved to alternative accommodation but the NIHE took no action against perpetrators, many of whom were known to be NIHE tenants. Effectively this rewarded sectarian violence and created new ghettos, further exacerbating Catholic–Protestant divisions in Northern Ireland (Graham, 1992).

In cultural policy, too, there were deep tensions between stated and unstated policy objectives. After the AIA, the Northern Ireland Office (NIO) became publicly committed to encouraging a pluralist culture in the North, in which the 'two traditions' of nationalism and unionism could coexist (Knox, 1992). This was expressed in a variety of community relations initiatives, which were aimed at increasing mutual cultural awareness, with the added bonus of improving the British state's image, both in Northern Ireland and abroad, further stabilising its legitimacy in the North. Partly as a consequence, cultural policies were also used to further marginalise and weaken expressions of mass, often politicised, Irishness. This process of cultural exclusion subjected Gaelic games organisations, voluntary organisations and parts of the Irish language movement to intensive monitoring and political vetting in order to ensure that the government could not be accused (by unionists) of assisting republican organisations (Ruane and Todd 1992b). In contrast, cultural organisations from the loyalist community, for instance from the Protestant-only Orange Lodges, were unquestioningly deemed to be legitimate expressions of Northern culture.

Furthermore, these various 'anti-sectarian' initiatives were established hand-in-hand with the denial of basic human rights in Northern Ireland. The British government actively encouraged an increasingly Protestant-dominated RUC and UDR to repress 'disloyal' republican communities. Throughout the first twenty-five years of Direct Rule, the government failed to take action either to reform or to disband elements of the security forces that had failed to secure broad acceptance in nationalist and republican communities. Indeed, such forces became more, not less, powerful, as under Direct Rule, they were made responsible to a single Junior Minister appointed by Westminster often for a short period of time and with no political base in Northern Ireland.

Meanwhile, the Northern Ireland legal framework was reformed in a way that increased the number of people prosecuted for 'terrorist' crime. The Emergency Provisions Act which replaced the Special Powers Act in 1973 established no-jury 'Diplock' courts. These were only required to rule confessional evidence as inadmissible if it could be proved that it had resulted from 'torture, inhuman or degrading treatment'. This was a clear incentive for the RUC and the army to pressurise prisoners into either incriminating themselves, or others. The result was that eighty-five per cent of convictions for 'terrorist offences' from 1973 were obtained on confessional evidence (Rowthorn and Wayne, 1988, p. 53–5). Not surprisingly, by 1992 Northern Ireland had a per capita prison population unrivalled anywhere in Western Europe (and in Eastern Europe matched only by that of Hungary), while it had one of the lowest per capita prison populations for 'non-scheduled', non-'terrorist' crime.[16]

Furthermore, the UK became the only EU state to seek permanent derogation from the European Convention on Human Rights, under Article 15, declaring that a 'national emergency' existed in the UK. Although in 1976, due to adverse publicity, the Convention was adopted in full, by 1988 the European Court's finding, that the Prevention of Terrorism Act breached the Convention, forced the government again to apply for exemption.[17] After Sinn Féin's decision to contest elections, the government's legislative armoury was further extended into political life: prisoners were banned from candidature in 1981, Republicans elected to the Northern Ireland Assembly were banned from entry into Britain in 1982, and in 1988, Republicans were prevented from speaking on UK television and radio. These and other measures made a nonsense of bodies such as the Standing Advisory Commission on Human Rights, set up in 1973, and the Police Complaints Authority, set up in 1987. Despite British government assurances that such bodies would ensure that 'emergency' powers and security concerns would not undermine civil rights, no prosecutions resulted from their deliberations. These agencies could not even act as 'window-dressing' as in over fifty per cent of cases, the army and the RUC refused to allow soldiers or police officers to participate in their inquiries, ostensibly for 'security' reasons (Rolston, 1987).

Despite Direct Rule, the British government was unable to secure political stability in the North. From the early 1980s, it returned to the option of seeking the South's assistance in maintaining stability, an approach that had been abandoned after unionist opposition to Sunningdale, and now was primarily seen as a means of isolating Sinn Féin. In 1984, discussions between the two governments were intensified, focusing on a range of proposals, such as a joint security commission and a police force for the whole island, an Anglo–Irish ministerial commission to deal with socio-economic and EU-related issues, and legal harmonisation with a Bill of Rights, 'mixed' courts and a legal Commission (Fitzgerald, 1991, p. 513). In return, the Irish government was willing to recognise de facto British sovereignty in Northern Ireland on the basis of Northern Irish popular consent.

These discussions posed a real dilemma for the British Conservative government – between its own understanding of British sovereignty and the need to offer some role for the Republic in the affairs of Northern Ireland. After protracted inter-governmental discussions, the Thatcher government drew a fine distinction between consultation on issues of common North–South concern, which, it was felt, would not impinge on British sovereignty – and joint authority, which was deemed unacceptable as it required a sharing of sovereignty between the two states. The nationalist Conservative Party then accepted this position largely because it would bring the Republic closer to the British government position, away from the influence of Sinn Féin. In 1985, following Mrs Thatcher's condemnation of the NIF report, the government adopted this minimalist consultative approach, under the AIA, carefully stipulating that any joint arrangements would have to be referred to as an Anglo–Irish 'Conference' rather than as a 'Commission' (which the British felt would have an undesired resonance in the EU).

In effect, Britain had admitted failure in building a settlement based on internal Northern Ireland structures. Instead, it had recruited the South as a partner to restabilise political relations in the North and to restore its tarnished international reputation.[18] The South also gained a diplomatic coup, enabling it to maintain Northern Ireland at arm's length while claiming to fulfil its obligations to Northern nationalists. At the same time the agreement enabled both states to more effectively, and more efficiently, prosecute the war against the IRA, which by 1993 had cost the Republic in excess of IR£2.5 billion, triple the per capita cost of the British government's anti-insurgency measures.[19]

This 'direct rule with a green tinge' established a form of institutionalised consultation, linked to 'implementing measures' that committed the British state to improving consociational arrangements in the North (Article 6) (O'Leary and McGarry, 1990, p. 279–81). On North–South issues there was to be improved cooperation in security matters, with the two separate police forces reporting to their respective governments. Only on matters relating to economic, social or cultural cooperation (not policing or judicial affairs) was there to be discussion of North–South cooperation through the joint Anglo–Irish Council. This limited space for North–South policy-making was itself to be created only 'if it prove(d) impossible to achieve and sustain devolution on a basis which secures widespread acceptance in Northern Ireland' (Article 10). This political bribe was aimed at persuading unionist politicians to accept power-sharing in the North; although it also recognised that such structures would be needed even in the event of devolution.

Britain's overall approach was outlined by the British Ambassador to the Republic, Sir Nicholas Fenn, in 1989. In the first instance, as the government had been claiming since 1972, he argued it was a neutral arbiter in the conflict and did 'not seek to impose a blueprint on the ultimate destiny of Northern Ireland'. Nevertheless, the government was fully prepared to protect the democratic rights of the unionist majority and to 'look at the law where it is open to abuse' by Republicans or Nationalists. This may require limitations on the right to silence for police suspects and on freedom of expression, including a requirement that those in public office sign a statement renouncing violence. At the same time, he argued the government should normalise politics, through fair employment legislation, community relations policies, fair housing allocation and even-handed policies on the administration of justice (Fenn, 1989, p. 57).

This combination of repression and reform expressed the inevitably contradictory pressures on the British government under Direct Rule. In the early 1980s, with the political success of Sinn Féin, these shaky foundations for political order began to break down and the British government was forced into accepting a greater role for the Republic in legitimising the political and social order in the North. This perhaps signalled a sea-change in state policies, North and South, and was a significant conditioning factor in the emerging negotiating agenda for the later 'peace process'.

Overall, there was sharp divergence in state policies, North and South in the first forty years of Partition. There was some symbolic and tentative convergence in the 1960s as both governments developed externally orientated economic policies. This was reversed with political implosion and Direct Rule in the North after 1972. British political priorities and British government finance came to dominate Northern government. Meanwhile, despite a reawakened interest in Northern issues, the Southern state remained relatively aloof, especially after the Sunningdale breakdown.

Yet, as successive British governments sought to construct political stability in the North, they were increasingly forced to accept a political role for the Republic in Northern affairs. This opened up new North–South political channels, expressing the Republic's renewed concern for political developments in the North following the emergence of Sinn Féin. Despite having little substantive effect on North–South linkages, these channels had significant symbolic impacts for both states. It can be argued that these could make further adjustments of state policies possible, North and South, if economic and political pressures encouraged closer North–South integration. The EU context for such a shift in state policies, North and South, is discussed in Chapter Four.

CONCLUSIONS

The Southern economy was deindustrialised in the nineteenth century and, partly as a consequence, the Southern state that emerged in the 1920s was dominated by a rural-based conservatism that shaped a protectionist, autarchic economic policy until the late 1950s. The North was industrialised in the late nineteenth century, producing for export on the basis of sectarianised labour relations, and the Northern statelet that emerged in 1921 was defined by continued membership of the UK, and by the socio-political domination of a nationalist minority. North–South divergence persisted until the late 1950s, with the 'carnival of reaction both North and South', which James Connolly had predicted would follow Partition (Berresford Ellis, 1988, p. 275).

This divergence was to some degree reversed in the mid-twentieth century with increased convergence in economic interests. Political relations in Northern Ireland, however remained firmly defined by confrontation with the South. This was reflected in Northern Ireland state policies, which were aimed at 'modernising' the North whilst shoring-up sectarian division between 'loyal' Protestants and 'disloyal' Catholics – itself an internal expression of North–South division. The failure to reconcile these competing objectives was a major factor in the reemergence of loyalist extremism, in the failure to satisfy the civil rights movement and in the eventual collapse of Stormont.

The result, in the 1970s, was a period of sharp political divergence. In the North, the loyalist DUP split off from the UUP, and the repression of the civil rights movement radicalised Northern nationalists, leading to the reemergence of an IRA committed to armed struggle. The imposition of Direct Rule, accompanied by the wholesale collapse of the Northern economy, and related dependence on the British Treasury, tied the North more closely to Britain. To a degree, this repressed tensions between economic interests and political conflict: employment was created for middle and upper working-class Protestants and for middle-class Catholics, and challenges to British authority were thereby concentrated in an increasingly marginalised Catholic working class. But the status quo was maintained at a price: in terms of on-going socio-political exclusion, particularly of the republican community; in terms of on-going militarisation of society in Britain and the Republic as well as in Northern Ireland; and in terms of an escalating Northern dependence on a British subvention, which was increasingly becoming, as the Secretary of State called it in 1993, 'an incentive for change' in British state policy. Meanwhile, the relatively peaceful South pursued an EU-orientated growth path and became increasingly dependent on EU markets and external capital.

In the 1980s and 1990s, there were some signals that the status quo, North and South, was becoming unsustainable. First, facing the decline of indigenously owned industry, economic élites began to suggest that the answer to Ireland's vicious circle of dependency and unemployment lay in greater North–South integration. Second, there was a reforging of all-island political perspectives, expressed in the deliberations of the NIF and the Hume–Adams 'peace process' a process of 'national reconciliation' that had the potential to encompass the Northern unionists. Third, the British and Irish governments rediscovered their joint interest in containing the conflict and in establishing Anglo–Irish and North–South institutions to manage their common political agendas. In the 1990s, with accelerated EU integration, the North–South context for economic interests, political conflict and state policy was intensifying. These EU related pressures are examined, respectively, in Chapters Two, Three and Four.

2

Interests: towards a 'single island economy'?

The deepening of European integration through the European Economic Community (EEC), the Single European Market (SEM) and the Economic and Monetary Union (EMU), is aimed at creating a deregulated 'economic space' amongst member states. In relatively peripheral economies, such as Ireland, North and South, there have been fears that the anticipated 'dynamic' effects of integration would pass them by. For these weaker regions, the EU is seen as job destroying, not job creating. But the fortunes of peripheral areas like Ireland are by no means determined by the EU's centrifugal tendencies. To meet the economic threat, many have argued for more interventionist policies implemented by local and regional bodies, and by the state, as well as by EU institutions, to enhance regional 'cohesiveness' (O'Donnell, 1991, p. 130). This has generated a debate on how best to maximise economic opportunities, and minimise threats, for Ireland North and South in the EU.

This chapter investigates these debates; first, it outlines some of the existing tendencies for North–South economic convergence and the emergence of increasingly intense demands, primarily from business interests, North and South, for increased integration. Second, these pressures for regional convergence are qualified by outlining the pressures for North–South economic divergence – pressures which reflect conflicting state priorities pursued by the UK and by the Republic of Ireland.

2.1 ISLAND–WIDE INTERESTS

In the 1990s, the two Irish economies were increasingly similar. Both were dependent on external sources of finance – the

55

Republic on EU funds and, to a greater extent, Northern Ireland on the British subvention. Both were also heavily reliant on agriculture and multinational branch plants. As industrial employment became less significant in Northern Ireland, service employment, both public and private, expanded in a process of 'demarketisation', as well as a process of deindustrialisation more common elsewhere in the EU.[1] The Republic continued to industrialise, with increased employment in capital-intensive multinational companies, and in the 1980s, there was a rapid growth of employment in the service industry, mirroring tendencies in the North.[2]

As illustrated in Table 2.1, this led to some considerable convergence in employment structures. In 1961, close to forty per cent of employees in the Republic were working in primary industry (principally agriculture), contrasting with thirteen per cent in Northern Ireland – a gap of twenty-seven per cent. By 1993, this had narrowed to ten per cent, reflecting increased secondary employment in the South combined with a declining Northern manufacturing. Indicators of living standards also converged.[3] As outlined in Table 2.2, the Republic began the 1970s with a per capita GDP roughly equal to Northern Ireland's. This had fallen to ninety-two per cent by 1980, only to recover some seventeen per cent by 1990. As GDP includes all profits and property income, regardless of whether they are repatriated or retained in Ireland, disposable income provides a more realistic measure of living standards. These figures are provided in Table 2.3, which also shows a significant narrowing of income differentials, from fifty-five per cent in 1975 to forty-eight per cent in 1980, and then, dramatically, to fourteen per cent in 1990. This occurred despite the increasing British subvention, which rose from twenty-three to thirty per cent of total expenditure in the North.[4]

Socio-economic convergence is also reflected in comparative figures. As illustrated in Table 2.4, Northern Ireland's per capita GDP deteriorated in comparison with EU average income levels by some five percentage points, while the Republic's position improved by nine points. Again, this presents an exaggerated picture of North–South convergence and contrasts with the relative figures for GNP per capita in the Republic which improved by some three percentage points, mirroring

Table 2.1 PERCENTAGE OF TOTAL EMPLOYMENT IN ECONOMIC
SECTORS, NORTH AND SOUTH

Employment	Northern Ireland			Republic of Ireland		
Sector	1961	1977	1993	1961	1977	1993
Primary	13.1	7.3	4.5	37.3	21.7	14
Secondary	40.4	38.5	28.3	23.7	32.4	29
Tertiary	46.5	54.2	67.2	39.0	45.9	57

NORTHERN IRELAND: EMPLOYMENT BY SECTOR, 1961–1993

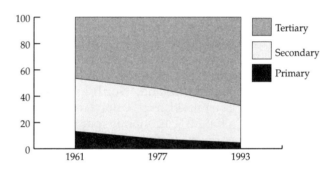

THE REPUBLIC: EMPLOYMENT BY SECTOR, 1961–1993

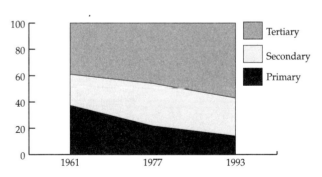

Source: Eurostat Regio Data.

Table 2.2 GDP PER CAPITA: NORTHERN IRELAND AND THE REPUBLIC

	1970	1980	1990
Northern Ireland (St£'000)	546	2,646	6,181
Republic (IR£'000)	549	2,752	7,423
Northern Ireland (ECU'000)	1,284	4,471	8,715
Republic (ECU'000)	1,306	4,100	9,524
GDP per capita in the Republic as a percentage of Northern GDP	101%	92%	109%

Source: European Economy; Northern Ireland Annual Abstract of Statistics; Eurostat (1993) National Accounts 1970–91.

the tendencies highlighted in Table 2.3. Converging living standards, i.e. downward convergence, are also reflected in rates of unemployment, which doubled in both economies in the late 1970s and early 1980s, as outlined in Table 2.5.

In many respects then, Ireland, North and South were becoming more peripheralised, as part of increasingly uneven development within the EU's 'economic space'. One result of rising unemployment was increased productivity in both parts of Ireland in the mid 1980s and early 1990s, rising by twenty-four per cent in Northern Ireland and by sixty-five per cent in the Republic between 1985 and 1993. Wage rates in the

Table 2.3 NET DISPOSABLE INCOME PER CAPITA, NORTH AND SOUTH

	1975	1980	1990
Northern Ireland (St£'000)	2,307	3,461	5,581
Republic of Ireland (IR£'000)	1,008	2,067	4,987
Northern Ireland (ECU'000)	4,106	5,849	7,590
Republic of Ireland (ECU'000)	1,833	3,085	6,561
Disposable income in the Republic as a percentage of Northern income	45%	52%	86%

Source: UK Regional Trends, HMSO; National Income and Expenditure, DSO; European Economy, 1992.

Table 2.4 RELATIVE PER CAPITA GDP AND GNP: PER CENT
OF EU AVERAGE

(EU=100, Purchasing Power Standard)	1973	1980	1990
GDP per capita: Northern Ireland	79	62	74
Republic	59	63	68
GNP per capita: Republic	59	62	62

Source: Matthews, 1994; Eurostat.

Republic fell by some fifteen per cent relative to other EU states and state subsidies for industry in both economies remained high: in the North, subsidies accounted for eighteen per cent of manufacturing GDP, the highest in the EU, comparing with thirteen per cent in the South, 0.5 per cent in England and 15.8 per cent in Italy. Yet still both North and South faced high levels of long-term 'structural' unemployment, officially at nine per cent, North and South, out of a total 14.5 per cent unemployed in the Republic and 13.4 per cent in Northern Ireland.

The implementation of EU funding régimes encouraged this convergence process. For instance, farmers, North and South tried to predict shifts in the agricultural support régimes, leading to convergence in the type of farming activity.[5] This was not mirrored in Britain, partly because of the greater dependence on agricultural support in the smaller, relatively unproductive farms in both parts of Ireland. EU regional policy had a similar effect as North and South were defined as priority regions for the Regional Development Fund; the Republic was defined as a region significantly 'lagging behind' other EU regions, while Northern Ireland, despite having a per

Table 2.5 PERCENTAGE OF THE WORKFORCE UNEMPLOYED,
NORTH AND SOUTH

	1970	1980	1990	1994
Northern Ireland	7.0	13.7	13.4	14.0
Republic of Ireland	6.3	8.0	14.5	18.7

Source: Eurostat.

capita GDP above the threshold for support as an 'Objective One' region, was granted the same funding status for 'special reasons'.[6]

These heightened similarities increased the awareness of a common interest in all-Ireland regional development. Despite EU regional funding, integration into the SEM was threatening the survival of indigenously owned industry, North and South. In Northern Ireland, it was estimated that forty-nine per cent of the region's private sector workforce was 'moderately vulnerable' to the removal of non-tariff barriers and to the expected increase in competition (Northern Ireland Economic Council (NIEC), 1992, p. 37). There were similar concerns in the Republic, leading the government to suggest that the task of creating a viable indigenous sector was 'the main common challenge facing industrial development, North and South' (DSO, 1992b, p. 41). Problems shared with the North included:

- high transport, communications and energy costs;
- weak marketing;
- low skill development, particularly in management skills;
- low levels of research and development;
- a lack of local sources of capital;
- and a sense of socio-political peripherality, particularly strong in the North.

Increased official concern was paralleled by heightened private sector merger activity. As elsewhere in the EU, there was an increase in cross-border North–South mergers and takeovers, in anticipation of the SEM. As outlined in Table 2.7, integration was particularly marked in private services. In the banking sector, for instance the Allied Irish Bank bought the Trustees Savings Bank in 1991, giving it a twenty-five per cent share of Northern banking, while the Ulster Bank increased its operations in the South and by 1993, accounted for ten per cent of the market in the Republic.[7] A similar process of capital concentration was underway in other sectors – a reorientation of ownership that was paralleled by changes in the marketing and pricing strategies of multinational companies, including Mars, Unilever, Marks and Spencer and Coca Cola, which began to treat Ireland as a single market.[8]

Table 2.6 ESTIMATES OF NORTHERN IRELAND PRIVATE SECTOR
EMPLOYEES WORKING IN ALL-IRELAND COMPANIES

	1993		1995	
	Numbers	%	Numbers	%
Manufacturing	2,252	2	8,124	8
Retail	12,659	12	15,892	15
Banking	4,708	11	11,177	27
Total private sector	27,626	8	46,319	13

Sources: Bord Tráchtála (Irish Trade Board) 1993 and 1995, *Market opportunities in Northern Ireland*, Appendix D, Dublin; 'Northern Ireland Top 100', *Belfast Telegraph*, 31 January, 1996; ('retail' includes distribution and hotels, 'banking' includes finance and insurance).

Overall, there was increased awareness that, in the context of the SEM, the development of the two economies would hinge on the ability to foster an indigenous industrial sector able to draw on combined mutual strengths. Prominent business leaders and government agencies, North and South, began arguing that if it was to do this, Irish business would have to formulate a new, all-Ireland framework for economic development. These pressures for North–South economic integration are examined in what follows, first from a Northern perspective.

The North

As elsewhere in the EU, the Northern Ireland economy was facing new and intensified competition in the SEM. This was combined with on-going industrial collapse and fear of public sector cutbacks. In 1993, the Confederation of British Industry in Northern Ireland (CBINI) estimated that an annual five per cent growth in GDP over the next decade would be needed for the region to reach the EU's average per capita wealth, whereas the highest growth achieved in the previous ten years had been only 2.5 per cent.[9] Similar concerns were expressed by the Irish Congress of Trade Unions (ICTU) which pointed out that in 1993, the number of people employed in manufacturing was less than the number registered as unemployed. Meanwhile, the public sector, the 'engine for job creation' in the North, was running out of steam (Barooah, 1993) and was threatening to go into reverse as the Conservative government tried to reduce the UK public deficit (EU funding, at 2.3 per cent of public expenditure in the North, offered no substitute).

The urgent need for a viable industrial strategy for the Northern economy in the Single Market was forcing Northern business to reassess and reorientate their economic interests, perhaps forcing the 'radical rethink of public policy' that some have argued is required (Hart and Harrison, 1992, p. 126). In 1989, the EU Commission suggested that the North was 'not entirely integrated into either the legal or the economic system of the UK' and concluded that 'it is therefore not really relevant to see it in a UK context'.[10] As the Coopers and Lybrand survey of Northern business stated in 1990, the North required an 'approach to the development of the Province different from that adopted in other regions of the UK'.[11] Traditionally, interests had been defined largely in terms of their UK setting and sometimes in the broader EU and international context, but rarely were they orientated to the South. A survey in 1992 for instance, found that forty-four per cent of Northern firms had never considered selling into the South.[12]

It was not until 1990 that the annual assessments of the Northern economy produced by the NIEC included an account of economic conditions in the Republic. Previously the Southern economy was considered so extraneous as not to deserve a specific mention in these lengthy yearly reports (NIEC, 1990, p. 6). This, perhaps, symbolic move by a semi-autonomous 'quango' stemmed from increased awareness of the significance of the South for Northern interests, reflecting what one prominent participant described as 'nothing short of a sea-change in economic relationships within the island' (Quigley, 1992, p. 4).

The visit of the Irish Taoiseach, Charles Haughey in April 1990, to a Northern Ireland Institute of Directors Conference was the first public indication of this reorientation in North–South business relations.[13] His message was that business, North and South, had to see the island as a single operating base and had to work together if it was to survive in the SEM. This was backed-up by a survey of cross-border cooperation

calling for initiatives on a sector-by-sector basis. The message
was well received and the Taoiseach was given no less than
three standing ovations from a thousand-strong audience of
Northern business people.[14]

From 1990, this North–South orientation gained widespread acceptance within the Northern business community
and was most clearly expressed by Dr George Quigley,
Chairman of the Ulster Bank and of the Northern Ireland
Institute of Directors when, in 1992, he proposed that 'Ireland,
North and South, should become one integrated "island economy" in the context of the Single European Market' (Quigley,
1992). In the first instance, it was argued that this would allow
greater North–South trade, of particular benefit to the North.
As highlighted by the President of the Confederation of Irish
Industry (CII) in the same year, Southern business sold one
third as much per capita in the North as it did in the South,
suggesting a possible tripling of sales for Southern business.
Meanwhile Northern Ireland industry sold one sixth as much
per capita in the South as it did in the North, suggesting a possible six-fold increase in sales.[15] As a result, Liam Connellan, the
CII Director-General estimated, perhaps over-optimistically,
that this could lead to a net increase in manufacturing sales of £3
billion, creating an additional 75,000 jobs in Ireland as a whole
(Northern Ireland Centre in Europe (NICE), 1993, p. 134).

Beyond this potential increase in trade, Dr Quigley argued
that there would be considerable advantages in joint working.
The areas of possible cooperation, outlined by him as early as
1989 included:

- joint ventures;
- joint marketing;
- joint trade missions and exhibitions;
- joint research on sectoral and trade issues;
- improved communication links;
- joint support facilities for education and training;
- shared infrastructure;
- joint environmental action;
- and joint public sector acquisitions and sales.[16]

He suggested, in February 1992, that the unified economy
should be supported by a special EU fund for projects agreed

jointly by the EU Commission and the two governments. This would provide a direct route to Brussels should powers be devolved to a Northern Ireland Assembly, and to facilitate the development of a Belfast–Dublin 'economic corridor' which had been 'artificially constrained' in the past.[17] In 1993, he argued that this had the potential to release new productive energies in Ireland, suggesting that 'it would be ludicrous to be part of a single European market post–1992 and fail to transform the island of Ireland into a single market, not simply to raise cross-border trade, but also to develop all-island economic, "synergies"'.[18]

Various other spokespersons for Northern industry supported proposals for North–South integration. Nigel Smyth, Director of the CBINI, argued in 1992 that the North–South division of Ireland damaged industry on both sides of the border and advocated all-island integration 'purely and simply because it makes sound economic sense'.[19] Six months later in a report outlining its preferences for the 1994–99 EU funding round, the Confederation of British Industry (CBI) advocated a joint North–South 'inter-regional partnership' as a 'key element' in the funding package, arguing that provision for training, marketing and research, transport, tourism and environmental improvements should be devised within an all-island framework. It supported Quigley's proposal for a North–South 'economic corridor' on the eastern seaboard, arguing that such initiatives would allow business to exploit 'the synergies brought about by the formation of a critical mass and the development of clustering activities', as well as 'breaking down the psychological barriers which result from the border'.[20]

The CBI report had been drawn up 'in conjunction with' the CII and subsequently the two business organisations embarked on a three-year initiative funded by the International Fund for Ireland to investigate the possible benefits of North–South cooperation. A Joint Council of forty representatives was established and steering groups were set up to guide the project, which involved 450 companies from North and South. Meanwhile, joint lobbying focused on the need for improved transport and energy links and for coordinated public procurement, while practical cooperation led to a significant amount of all-Ireland import substitution in aerospace, textiles, pharmaceutical products and scientific instruments, and led to joint marketing strategies to win EU contracts in civil engineering and construction.[21] In the longer term, the intention was to assist Irish companies to compete within the island market and gain the resources, skills and confidence to sell in wider EU markets. These initiatives were seen in many quarters as offering a lifeline for Northern industry, as the project's coordinator, William Poole, argued, 'senior people North and South consider the initiative to be of high significance to the future prosperity of Irish industry'.[22]

The CBI's approach was clarified in 1993 when the director outlined seven strategic priorities for Northern Ireland if it was to aspire to 'world class' status, rather than remaining 'at the bottom of the UK league'. The director emphasised that strengthened linkages with the UK would not deliver the required upgrading of standards, while the development and implementation of strategic, mutually beneficial 'win-win' linkages in 'synergy' with the Republic offered an alternative, potentially highly rewarding development path, given that 'we cannot afford to continue on the track we are on'. These linkages could yield increased investment, reskilling and vocational training, improvements in innovation through technological partnerships, infrastructural development and marketing, particularly of Ireland's environmental qualities.[23]

The Northern Ireland Chambers of Commerce adopted a similar stance. The president, Noel Stewart, stated in 1992 that his organisation was 'at the forefront of initiatives to develop cross border links', primarily with their counterparts in the Republic.[24] The Belfast and Dublin Chambers of Commerce took joint initiatives to improve North–South cooperation including trade fairs and business conventions and drew up joint proposals for North–South projects. In 1993, they presented a joint paper to the Commission calling for trade-boosting projects, and outlined plans for setting up a 'Chamberlink' to encourage North–South investments. They were joined by the Northern agency for small firms, the Local Enterprise Development ment Unit (LEDU), which organised several conferences for cross-border business in 1992, arguing that economic 'survival lay first and foremost in togetherness'.[25]

These various initiatives reflected a widespread and relatively new consensus on the need for all-Ireland economic integration. In 1993, a survey found that ninety-seven per cent of Northern Ireland chief executives viewed North–South integration as either necessary (sixty-one per cent) or useful (thirty-six per cent), quoting one as saying 'there is no reason why Ireland should not operate as a single political and economic entity'.[26] This reorientation was by no means restricted to the business community. The ICTU, for instance, fearing the impact of the neo-liberal SEM, had argued for such an economic strategy as early as 1988, and in 1994 the ICTU president advocated government action to improve North–South links.[27] The Northern Ireland Council for Voluntary Action, the North's officially recognised voluntary sector umbrella body, also supported such action and in 1992, its director, Quintin Oliver, stressed the widespread, cross-community acceptance of the need to develop a single market in Ireland as a whole before being able to compete effectively in the SEM.[28]

There was a growing perception that the North, as the smaller of the two economies (population only 1.5 million, as compared to the South's 3.5 million), and without its own direct government representation in Brussels, was fast becoming 'a periphery of a periphery' (Anderson and Shuttleworth, 1993). Growing demands for government action to rectify this appeared to fall on deaf ears. Business organisations including the Chambers of Commerce were active in encouraging local authorities to take a more active role in the face of what Noel Stewart described as a 'remote, ponderous and largely unresponsive' central government.[29] Such organisations joined with local government in financing the NICE, with eighteen of Northern Ireland's twenty-six councils agreeing to finance the Centre. The Centre had staff in Belfast and Brussels and to some extent compensated for the North's indirect Whitehall route to Brussels, although it had no official status and was restricted to political lobbying.[30]

Overall, both sides of industry and especially the trade unions feared that the deregulated, neo-liberal SEM could have an extremely damaging impact, and argued that integration with the Southern economy offered a much needed lifeline for the Northern economy. This led to demands that the two governments establish North–South institutional frameworks to deliver economic integration, which had deep political implications for the national conflict. The conflict tended to 'asphyxiate' these North–South initiatives (Hainsworth, 1981, p. 14), and no doubt reflecting this, business enthusiasts for integration were at pains to be 'non-political'. But despite this, there were indications, particularly post–1992, that the shifts in economic orientation were forcing limited adaptations in the party-political positions and in state policies (these are discussed in Chapters Three and Four).

The South

As in Northern Ireland, EU membership posed a profound challenge, particularly to domestically owned firms in the Republic which were dependent on UK or home markets. As outlined in chapter one, there had been concerns at the lack of indigenous industrial development in the Republic for some years. Despite the 1970s disruption in international economic development, the flow of overseas investment into the Republic was maintained until the early 1980s. But in the meantime, indigenous industry went into rapid decline, only to recover, very marginally, in the late 1980s. From 1973, indigenous producers had faced intense competition for domestic markets, stimulating much intra-industry realignment, mostly against the EU tendency for economic concentration, and more towards greater fragmentation. This perhaps reflected the relative weakness of home owned industry in the Republic and presaged a more thorough-going inter-industry 'restructuring', or rather dismantling, in the context of recession in the first half of the 1980s.

Given that the entire period of EU membership had seen an 'almost continuous output and employment decline' in Irish owned industry, further deregulation in the SEM was viewed with some trepidation (NESC, 1989). Irish owned industry remained concentrated in low profit, largely agri-industrial sectors with relatively low technological input, dependent upon Southern Irish markets for over sixty per cent of production. In contrast, multinational and transnational companies maintained high profit rates (usually at least triple the rates in

Irish owned industry), and were orientated to external markets for seventy per cent of their sales and relied on non-Irish producers for seventy per cent of their inputs (O'Hearn, 1993, p. 179–82).

In some ways, lacking a stable source of external support equivalent to the North's subvention from its 'kind auntie', the British Treasury, there was less room for manoeuvre in the Southern economy than in Northern Ireland (Clulow and Teague, 1993, p. 102). EU funding, at 2.7 per cent of the Republic's GDP in 1993, although significant, was not sufficient to meet the Republic's needs or to compensate for the deflationary capital drain caused by Irish membership of the ERM. In the early 1980s, unemployment had doubled, to eighteen per cent, comparable or even higher than in Northern Ireland. Wage levels were substantially lower than in most other EU countries and had become lower in the 1980s without a commensurate rise in employment with indigenously owned companies.

In the face of industrial weakness and dependent development within a twenty-six county framework, there were greater demands for 'positive' integration at the EU level and at the all-Ireland level. A concern for systems of regional or 'national' innovation, for integrated institutional structures as well as for integrated economic sectors – defining economic development as irreconcilably interrelated with political development – came to dominate thinking on approaches to stimulating indigenous development (NESC, 1989; Mjoset, 1993). Some argued that the South had been naïve to believe that a deregulated EU would deliver prosperity. As one newspaper pointed out in 1993, 'by joining the rich man's club we hoped to become rich' – what one southern Member of the European Parliament (MEP) described as an 'Alice in Wonderland' approach; instead the EU had 'strengthened the community's economic centre relative to the periphery'.[31]

There was on-going dissatisfaction with what was seen as a policy of attracting overseas capital while indigenous industry suffered.[32] In the immediate post-Maastricht period, rising unemployment, the forced devaluation of the Punt, the increased incidence of 'social dumping' by multinational companies, the reduced supply of foreign investment, the failure to meet the so-called Maastricht 'convergence criteria' and the impending reduction in EU structural funding, forced the issue of indigenous development, in an island economy, higher up the political agenda. Meanwhile, linkages with other peripheral regions or states, such as Spain and Portugal and Greece, to pressurise for firmer 'cohesion' policies in the EU became more significant.

As in the North, all-island integration was, to a great extent, seen as a means of reversing economic stagnation.[33] Like the North, indigenous industry in the Republic was primarily linked to domestic and British markets. Southern exports to Britain were dominated by the products of the largely home owned agri-industry (channelled through Belfast, which in 1988 took fifty-eight per cent of the Republic's cargo traffic) (DSO, 1992b). Hence, attempts at stimulating indigenous industry in the South necessarily had to draw on the North's as well as the South's economic capabilities, building upon the common orientations of the two economies to British markets as well as to each other. Indeed, if economic development was to be redefined as 'indigenous', 'regional' development, it necessarily had to become an all-island, thirty-two county concern, rather than simply a matter for the twenty-six county Republic (NESC, 1989).

Common concerns in agri-industry included quality control, joint price support mechanisms, joint marketing, production quotas, disease control and rural development in border areas. By 1993, the Irish Trade Board (ITB) was participating in joint international trade fairs with the Northern Ireland Industrial Development Board (IDB) and was joining the ITB in calling for EU funds to establish an 'island network of communication and transport'.[34] The need to improve linkages between multinational industry and local suppliers was also defined as an all-Ireland issue; this was the focus, for instance, of a series of subcontractors' exhibitions, organised by the ITB and the IDB in 1992.[35]

Yet in many ways there was less Southern enthusiasm for North–South integration, partly because it had direct access to EU structures and had been able to negotiate a major, although one-off, contribution from EU structural funds for the period from 1994 to 1999 under the 'Cohesion' Fund. This may have reflected a 'businessman's dole mentality' in the Republic, given the yearly IR£1.5 billion in tax breaks and high level of industrial grants in the South.[36] More likely, given that such grants were set at a higher level in Northern Ireland, the larger Southern business sector saw itself in open competition with the North, and in any case set its sights on EU markets rather than on the smaller all-Ireland market. These pressures for inter-capitalist North–South competition rather than collaboration are examined below in the next sub-section.

Overall, in the early 1990s, the need for economic strategies aimed at generating indigenous development in Ireland, North and South, was increasingly being recognised. The *Irish Times* argued in an editorial in 1992 that the 'economic case for closer cooperation is compelling' (DSO 1992b).[37] Fear for Ireland's economic future in the deregulated SEM was leading to a reassessment of economic interests and was stimulating demands for North–South inter-regional integration to jointly build on Ireland's economic strengths (Anderson and Shuttleworth, 1993). As the Northern nationalist-orientated *Irish News* commented in 1993, 'during the last 12 months it has become increasingly clear that the concerns of Irish business North and South are virtually identical'; and significantly, the more unionist-orientated *Belfast Telegraph* agreed, arguing that the process of EU integration was bringing North and South closer together as 'the island is too small for the two states to go it alone'.[38]

Business interests North and South were realising that without economic integration on the 'island of Ireland', both parts of the economy would fail to remain competitive in the SEM. This regionalisation of economic interests in Ireland was directly related to the process of EU integration and was leading to the formation, or rather reformation, of an all-Ireland middle class. In the 1990s, business classes began demanding political action to develop the 'island economy' – demands that had clear implications for the positions of political parties and for state policies. These are discussed in Chapter Three and Chapter Four below, but first the on-going, and in some cases increased, North–South economic divisions are discussed.

2.2 DIVIDED INTERESTS

'Regional' convergence has to be set against on-going, and in some cases sharpened, 'national' divergence between North and South. This can largely be attributed to the upsurge in national conflict, centred on the North, and to a lesser extent to competition between the two parts of Ireland, especially for sources of inward investment. Unlike the case in Northern Ireland, by the later 1970s Britain had ceased to be the 'origin and destination of most trade, capital and labour' in the Republic (O'Cleireacain, 1983, p. 109). While the South increasingly defined itself as a region of the EU, the North became more, not less, dependent on the UK economy, primarily in terms of its dependence on the British Treasury.

The two economies and societies were poorly integrated. In a sense, people living in the two parts of Ireland shared 'a small island with their backs firmly turned on each other'.[39] The inadequacy of road, rail and telephone links reflected political and social divisions, not just between unionists and nationalists, but also between a war-torn North and a relatively peaceful South.[40] Reflecting the development priorities of the British government and on-going dependence of the North on London based financial markets, the Northern Ireland IDB remained primarily orientated to finding market 'niches' in the British economy and to attracting British multinationals. As the Director of the CBI argued in 1992, UK companies had moved to the region to take advantage of fewer skill shortages, lower wage costs and low staff turnover, giving them 'a critical competitive advantage' in British markets.[41]

Meanwhile, common dependence on multinational capital, North and South, did not in itself imply common interests. On the contrary, the two regions competed for international capital, through the IDA in the South and the IDB in the North, and multinational producers rarely had local linkages, despite some North–South convergence in marketing and pricing strategies. This competition to attract increasingly scarce and footloose international capital was seen as mutually damaging, not least as it diverted public finances and policy initiatives away from the more sustainable indigenous sector.[42]

The direct public funding of 'industrialisation by invitation', stood at £103 million sterling in the North for the period 1986–92, while in the South IR£429 million was paid to overseas firms 1981–90. Many of these companies then benefited from tax breaks, training and infrastructure grants, which in the South added up to an estimated IR£600 million in 1991 (DSO, 1992a; Hamilton, 1993). As early as 1983, the Permanent Secretary to the Northern Ireland Department of Economic Development highlighted this competition as a barrier to North–South cooperation.[43] By 1993, competition had intensified as sources of international capital began to dry up in the post–1989 context of deregulation in the former Communist countries of East and Central Europe. In that year, for instance, the Northern IDB deliberately out-bid the Southern IDA to attract a Malaysian textile plant, Hualon, and in attracting a US Battery plant, Valance, to the North.

For multinationals as well as for local firms, there were many barriers to North–South linkages, including poor transport links, uncertainty in currency exchange rates and a lack of knowledge of suppliers and markets across the border. Northern companies with 'parents' in Britain tended to price their goods and services at rates reflecting British rather than local circumstances although, as mentioned earlier, there were some indications that this was changing in the early 1990s.[44] At the same time, reflecting the increasing concentration of economic power within the EU and increased investment opportunities outside the EU, there was a marked increase in 'social dumping'. Perhaps the most disruptive disinvestment in the Republic was the departure, one year after the completion of the SEM, of the electronics firm, Digital, which had employed 1,500 technicians in Galway – a relocation which stimulated widespread questioning of the Republic's dependency on externally determined economic decisions.[45]

In addition, as well as being dependent on inward investment, the North, and to a lesser degree the South, were, and still are, dependent on continued fiscal redistribution. While there was a degree of shared dependence on EU funding régimes, leading to joint working on EU funding issues, the North was considerably more dependent on sources of funds from the British Treasury, which dwarfed EU expenditure. In

1990, EU funding accounted for 10.8 per cent of public expenditure in the Republic while in the North, as noted earlier, it accounted for 2.3 per cent.[46] While clearly insufficient, the funds provided a useful boost to investment in the Republic, raising gross fixed capital formation by 6.3 per cent to 17.9 per cent of GDP in 1989, comparing with an EU average of 20.6 per cent (CEC, 1990, p. 73). The North, meanwhile, as noted earlier, was dependent on the UK Treasury subvention for a third of its GDP.

In 1993, the issue of EU funding had become an election issue in the South as politicians strove to maximise both the size of the structural funds 'cake' and the Republic's slice of it. In the North, by contrast, the UK Treasury was the focus of concern. As the Secretary of State stated, the EU allocation of £1,040 million sterling to Northern Ireland for the period 1994–99 'reflect[ed] the very special needs of the region' and complemented the government's subvention to the North which was expected to amount to at least £18,000 million sterling over the same period.[47]

Beyond these structural and fiscal dimensions, there remained deep divisions between business élites, North and South, founded on mutual fears and suspicions – a legacy of many decades of national conflict which officials from the Northern Ireland LEDU defined as the main barrier to integration.[48] Diverging economic policies of the Republic and the UK led to virtually separate economic development in an already divided island, and while the economic base had become more similar, this was the result not of convergence, but of divergence, as the North 'demarketised' while the South industrialised.

The South

EU integration allowed the Republic to weaken its dependence on the UK economy, reflecting the effects of increased overseas investment in the Republic and leading to substantial macroeconomic divergence between the two Irish economies (Blackwell and O'Malley, 1983).[49] In contrast with domestic owned industry, which remained highly dependent on Irish domestic and UK markets, multinational capital was orientated towards wider EU markets.

Table 2.7 DESTINATION AND SOURCE OF TRADE
IN THE REPUBLIC OF IRELAND

Destination of exports: percentage of total

	1960	1972	1981	1991
UK	75	61	43	36
Other EU countries	6	17	32	41
Non-EU countries	19	22	25	23

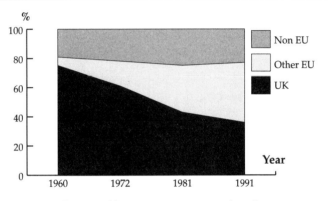

Source of imports: percentage of total

	1960	1972	1981	1991
UK	49	51	51	42
Other EU countries	14	18	20	24
Non-EU countries	37	31	29	34

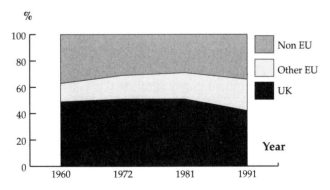

Source: McAleese, 1984 p. 161 and DSO Trade Statistics, 1992.

74

As a result, as illustrated in Table 2.7, from the 1960s the Republic's export markets were becoming increasingly non-British. This tendency was not so clear for imports which remained closely linked to British sources. In part, this reflected extensive transfer pricing by multinational corporations, as well as on-going penetration of the Republic's domestic market by British manufacturers.

Although this process of trade reorientation had begun in the 1960s, it accelerated from 1973 so that in 1982, for the first time, non-UK EU markets were more important than UK markets for exporters in the Republic (Harrison, 1990). This had clear implications for the Republic's economic relationship with the North, which remained tied to UK markets due to the relative absence of non-UK multinational capital. Exports to Northern Ireland became less important in the Republic; as illustrated in Table 2.8, cross-border exports fell as a percentage of GDP from 3.7 per cent in 1960 to 2.2 per cent in 1972, and in the context of increased exports overall they only partially recovered to 3.3 per cent in 1991. Reflecting this, as illustrated in Table 2.9, by the 1980s, exports to Northern Ireland had fallen as a percentage of overall exports by approximately a third (as had imports, to a lesser extent).

Macro-economic policy in the Republic expressed these shifting economic orientations. Given the small size of its economy and its extreme exposure to international trade, it was generally recognised that the Republic needed to align its currency with a larger partner. Until the 1970s, dependence on UK markets dictated that the Sterling link be retained, but with EU membership and strengthened trading relations with non-UK EU economies, it was preferable to build closer financial links with EU money markets. From the early 1970s, the

Table 2.8 REPUBLIC OF IRELAND EXPORTS TO THE NORTH PERCENTAGE OF GDP.

	1960	1972	1991
Overall exports	30.6	33.2	59.7
Exports to Northern Ireland	3.7	2.2	3.3

Source: European Economy; *Belfast Telegraph*, 8 June 1993.

Table 2.9 NORTH–SOUTH TRADE: TOTAL VOLUME AND AS
A PERCENTAGE OF TOTAL IMPORTS FROM AND EXPORTS
TO NORTHERN IRELAND

IR£ million	1980	1990	1992
Imports from Northern Ireland	223.5 (4.1)	500.1 (3.0)	486.2 (3.6)
Exports to Northern Ireland	300.4 (7.4)	816.5 (5.7)	825.1 (4.9)

Source: DSO Trade Statistics 1992, 1994.

Republic began to use the Euro-currency market to finance balance-of-payments deficits and as a source of public borrowing, rather than relying on the City of London, and by 1979, only two per cent of the Republic's foreign debt was denominated in Sterling (Bradley and Whelan, 1992).

This was followed by the Republic's decision to de-link the Punt from Sterling in 1979, and to join the ERM. Pegging the Punt to Sterling had forced the Republic to shadow UK growth rates which in the 1970s were significantly more inflationary than the rest of the EU. The new ERM link was seen as providing a more deflationary anchor for the Republic, as well as reflecting its increasingly EU orientated industrial base. The Punt was pegged to the Deutschmark-dominated ECU, effectively transforming macro-policy and providing a new 'sheet anchor' for the economy (see Chapter One). As the UK failed to join the ERM until 1990 (and then only for two years), 1979 marked the effective end of over 150 years of monetary union with the UK.

As a result, as illustrated in Figure 2.10 (p. 78), there was considerable divergence between Punt and Sterling rates of exchange throughout the 1980s. After joining the ERM, the Punt depreciated slightly until 1987 when it stabilised at ECU 1.29. This contrasted with the Sterling rate, which appreciated between 1978 and 1982 from ECU 1.56 to 1.78 to the Pound in 1982. The two exchange rates converged after the UK joined the ERM in 1990 and subsequently as Sterling shadowed the emerging 'Euro'.

ERM membership was followed by a period of instability as monetary, fiscal and income policies were reorientated away from UK tendencies to more closely mirror the policies of other ERM members (O'Donnell, 1993a, p. 70). Falling output and rapidly increasing unemployment (from seven per cent to seventeen per cent between 1980 and 1985) led to a breakdown in corporatist economic management with trade deficits combined with high levels of public borrowing (3.5 per cent in 1983 and eight per cent in 1986).[50] Policies were reorientated with a rapid reversal of the fiscal reflation of 1979–81, and by the mid 1980s, a stable balance of payments was restored, with Irish interest rates and inflation rates mirroring German rather than UK rates (European Economy, 1994; O'Brien, 1993).

Again in contrast with UK tendencies, the role of corporatist, tripartite agreements was strengthened in the later 1980s. After the success of the 1987 *Programme for National Recovery*, which stabilised public finances as well as pay demands, such agreements came to play a central role in policy making. In 1991, the *Programme for Economic and Social Progress* updated these objectives and significantly was aimed at meeting the needs of Irish indigenous companies in the context of the Single Market, drawing on the experience of similar Western European economies (Mjoset, 1993; NESC, 1989).

This economic reorientation, bringing the Republic more into line with wider EU rather than with UK trends, led to wide divergences between the North and South. The break between the Punt and Sterling weakened North–South financial ties and was reflected in North–South price differentials, leading to a surge in cross-border shopping in the 1980s, mostly from South to North as Sterling fluctuated relative to the Punt in the mid 1980s. For the same reasons, cross-border smuggling increased as 'Monetary Compensation Amounts' (MCAs) could be earned by moving agricultural produce across the border.

As Sterling began to depreciate in the mid 1980s, ERM membership also temporarily damaged the Republic's competitiveness relative to the UK. Ironically, allowing the Punt to shadow Sterling – for instance in the period from 1970 to 1978 when it depreciated relative to other EU currencies – may have been of greater benefit to Irish indigenous producers than ERM membership (NESC, 1989). Nonetheless, in an economy dominated by multinationals, these and other factors such as the reduction in public borrowing, cuts in real wage levels and labour-shedding in Irish owned industry, boosted overall industrial productivity. This only served to further underscore North–South divergence since, from the mid 1980s to the early 1990s, industrial productivity in the Republic rose at twice the rate of productivity growth in Northern Ireland.[51]

The net effect was that from the late 1980s, economic fortunes in the Republic began to mirror those in the rest of the EU rather than in Britain and Northern Ireland. In previous years, the direction, if not the magnitude, of economic growth in the Republic tended to reflect shifts in the British economy rather than shifts experienced in other, similar EU economies. This pattern was reversed in the 1980s, leading to significant economic divergences between the Republic and Northern Ireland, with a discernable effect on North–South relationships. Cross-border shopping and smuggling led to tighter border controls and, in the case of the Republic, firmer customs

Figure 2.10 EXCHANGE RATES OF PUNT AND STERLING: VALUE OF £ST AND £IR MEASURED IN ECU 1978–1994

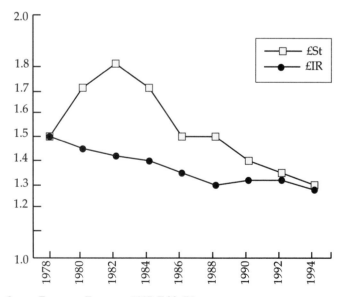

Source: European Economy, 1995, Table 56.

regulations, leading some to suggest that EU membership had 'emphasised the economic existence of an Irish border which was largely absent hitherto' (Trimble, 1989a, p. 43).

The North

Equally, economic interests in the North were by no means set in an all-Ireland framework, despite the enthusiasm for North–South integration. In the 1980s, the South became marginally more important to Northern exporters. Exports rose as a percentage of Northern GDP, from 2.9 per cent in 1972 to 4.7 per cent in 1991.[52] However, this reflected an overall reduction in the North's trading relations with non-Irish markets rather than a significant reorientation towards the South. In 1990, the Northern Ireland Economic Research Council estimated that Northern Ireland exports to the Republic accounted for approximately six per cent of total sales, while sales in Britain accounted for forty per cent. In terms of manufacturing exports, 9.4 per cent of Northern Ireland exports were destined for the Republic and 49.6 per cent to Britain, while 20.6 per cent were exported to other EU countries.[53]

Not surprisingly, UK macro-policies diverged from policies in the Republic. Perhaps in recognition of the special conditions existing in Northern Ireland, British government fiscal and industrial policies were applied with some care in Northern Ireland: the poll tax that was introduced in Scotland in 1989 and in Wales and England in 1990, was never implemented in Northern Ireland; Northern Ireland did not experience the public expenditure cuts of other UK regions – expenditure on the health service and on public housing remained significantly higher than in England throughout the 1980s; and the privatisation programme of the Thatcher government was not extended to Northern Ireland until well after her departure from government, with the listing of Northern Ireland electricity and water on the London stock markets in 1993.

Despite this relative isolation from British government policy shifts, the Northern economy was undermined by British macro-policies more orientated towards the interests of the City of London than to the needs of a region with a weak indigenous industrial sector on the periphery of the SEM. As the NIEC repeatedly pointed out, UK economic policy was orientated to meeting the needs of the UK macro-economy; not to the specific needs of the Northern Ireland economy (NIEC, 1989, p. 56; 1990, p. 46). This not only had a detrimental effect on the Northern economy but also undermined North–South linkages.

From 1979, for instance, UK fiscal policy was aimed at reducing rates of direct taxation and reducing the cost of labour, which, if anything, undermined the Northern economy as historically it had competed with British regions on the basis of relatively low wages for unskilled labour. Deregulation of labour markets, in contrast with the shift towards corporatism in the Republic, and falling wage rates in Britain reduced the comparative advantage of Northern Ireland, so damaging its relative productivity. Also as a result of deregulation, planning in Northern Ireland was disjointed and ad hoc, reacting to the on-going weakness of the Northern economy and reflecting the failure to embrace economic planning in the wider UK economy, despite bouts of recession in the late 1970s and 1980s.

This was also reflected in monetary policy, which in the UK was not so much 'counter-cyclical' as 'pro-cyclical'. This exacerbated the international business cycle to maintain the position of the City of London in global capital markets, with the by-product of undermining economic development in the UK's more peripheral regions. The application of monetarist policies led to high interest rates during the recession of the early 1980s; the response to the 1987 stock market crash led to low interest rates during the late 1980s recovery and the fear of 'over-heating' led to high interest rates in the recession of the early 1990s. The Northern economy was tied to what were often inappropriate monetary policies and it was systematically disadvantaged in relation to other, more central, regions of the UK, particularly in terms of the availability and cost of borrowing as Northern Ireland borrowers were required to pay a premium of up to three per cent on loans, reflecting the region's distance from the sources of UK financial power (NIEC, 1982, p. 122).

In addition, UK exchange rate policy did not provide Northern Ireland with the stable, preferably low, currency rate that it needed. UK entry into the ERM in 1990 at an overvalued Sterling to ECU rate, designed to favour British interests in the City of London, was followed by a period of severe exchange rate instability after the UK left the ERM in 1992. The devalued Sterling rate no doubt favoured Northern industry in subsequent years, but once again the UK Pound was subject to rapid fluctuations, independent of relative exchange rate stability in the Republic and the rest of the EU.

CONCLUSIONS

Facing concentration of economic power at the EU level, integration into the SEM increased the importance of developing viable, indigenously owned industry in the peripheral regions in the EU. In Ireland this forced business, North and South, to reorientate their interests – in the case of Northern Ireland, away from a UK-centred perspective, in the case of the Republic, away from an externally focused perspective, and in both parts of Ireland, towards an all-island perspective. It was no accident that this reorientation, and the political pressures that it placed on politicians, North and South, intensified in the early 1990s, so that by 1994 the need for an all-Ireland economic strategy had virtually become conventional wisdom.

There were, however, substantial economic obstacles to the formation of a single island economy, many of them directly related to EU integration. While the SEM encouraged greater integration between Northern Ireland and the Republic, it also strengthened the power of international capital at the EU level, leading to increased competition between the still externally orientated IDA and IDB. In the Republic, on-going, and indeed, increased dependence on externally owned industry, as indigenously-owned industry continued to decline, sharpened its dependence on EU markets and encouraged a more complete integration into EU financial and exchange markets, most clearly expressed in the Republic's membership of the ERM from 1979.

In Northern Ireland, continued disinvestment by multinational capital and the collapse of private, locally owned industry accelerated the process of 'demarketisation' and accentuated the region's dependence on the UK Treasury. At the same time, British economic policies remained geared towards maintaining the global influence of the City of London and, from 1979, towards defining the UK economy as a low-wage, deregulated location for multinational capital seeking access to EU markets. British financial autonomy from the EU was maximised, as was the ability to pursue a strategy of competitive deregulation, expressed in the UK opt-out from EMU and from the Social Protocol in the Maastricht Treaty. As EU integration accelerated and the fault-line between 'EU-sceptic' and 'EU-enthusiast' became more clearly defined in policy terms, the economic border between the Republic and Northern Ireland in some respects became more important.

These divergences suggested that if the presumed benefits of integration were to be realised for Ireland, North and South, there would need to be concerted political guidance and democratic involvement. The degree to which this was reflected in ideological shifts within Northern Ireland and the Republic and was translated into state-led, all-Ireland initiatives depended crucially on the process of mediation between economic shifts, ideological conflict and state policies. The following two chapters attempt to highlight this mediation, focusing on the relatively separate and autonomous dynamics of party-political conflict and state authority.

3

Ideologies: parties in conflict and consensus

In the context of the economic shifts outlined in the previous chapter, EU integration also stimulated ideological shifts, moving to a degree, the political framework away from conflicts over 'national' issues and towards conflicts over 'regional' issues. This chapter weighs up these contending regionalist and nationalist pressures. First, there is an attempt to assess the emerging, EU-related pressures towards consensus on the question of North–South regional integration in Ireland. Second, the on-going and in some cases strengthened pressures towards national divergence are examined.

Some political commentators have argued that EU integration would dispose of the 'sovereignty-identity obsession' in Ireland, offering the possibility of a 'reassessment of all relationships on these islands', weakening the conflict between British 'integration' and Irish 'separatism', and forging a new 'European citizenship'.[1] In this 'regionalist' model, it is argued that the weakening of state sovereignty in the EU strikes at the heart of the national conflict. As socio-economic issues are articulated in a common EU frame of reference in Ireland, North and South, it is possible to conceive of a redefinition of social interests, leading to a positive-sum 'synergy of positive collaboration' between North and South in Ireland.[2] This non-national, regional agenda for North–South unity emerged as the rhetoric of Ireland's politicians converged on EU-related issues, possibly replacing the 'tired slogans' of national conflict.[3] In the EU context, the constitutional question would be transformed from a zero-sum into a positive-sum issue, in which it is possible to conceive of EU and North–South dimensions as additional to Northern Ireland's status as part of the UK. This *de facto* federalism within the EU may 'reposition' Northern

Ireland in a set of European contexts, 'guaranteeing democratic participation and minority rights, economic development and cultural diversity'.[4]

There are, however, serious problems with these arguments, primarily as they assume that the transnational context can supersede relations between a dominant national political culture and its subordinates. Such denationalising, even if successful, would not necessarily address the roots of the conflict. Indeed, interpreting the conflict between Britain and the Republic over Northern Ireland as a relatively benign relationship between British 'integration' and Irish 'separatism' underestimates the historical and contemporary roots of the conflict and downplays the degree of ideological divergence between nationalism and unionism within Ireland. While all-Ireland regional integration may have become an economic necessity, this appeared to be having, at most, a minimal impact on the continuing pressures for ideological divergence in Ireland. Nonetheless, such 'regionalising' impacts may have longer term significance, and are examined in some detail in the next sub-section.

3.1 CONVERGING REGIONALISMS

EU institutions have played a key ideological role in legitimising the redefinition of Ireland as a single island rather than two separate jurisdictions. This has involved a redefinition of territory as EU institutions have sought to use depoliticised 'regional' concepts, free from national connotations – unlike existing terms associated with various shades of 'green' or 'orange', such as 'Ireland', 'Northern Ireland', the 'North of Ireland', 'Ulster', the 'Republic', the Free State, Éire, the Six and the Twenty-six counties.

In the early 1980s for instance, the Commission began using the concept of the 'totality of relations within these islands' as a single Irish and British geographical entity. This defined Northern Ireland as a matter of legitimate concern for the Republic as well as for Britain, and was initially floated by nationalist politicians in the South, in particular by Garret Fitzgerald (1972). The concept was developed at the EU level primarily because it allowed British and Irish representatives to discuss common issues on the sidelines of EU meetings, resulting in joint communiqués which could be released without the fear that either government would be accused of interfering in the other's 'sovereign' territorial jurisdiction. This provided the basis for inter-governmental Anglo–Irish dialogue on the North, a process of consultation and cooperation that culminated in the Anglo–Irish Agreement.[5]

In the later 1980s, the concept of the 'island of Ireland' became more current. This was used by the Commission as short-hand for the 'Republic of Ireland and Northern Ireland', as the Commission had been criticised for using the term 'Ireland' for the twenty-six county Republic. This issue was highlighted in the first session of the EP in 1979 by the UUP MEP John Taylor, who argued that the term 'Ireland' rubbed out the existence of the North.[6] Nationalists and Republicans had also criticised this habit of collapsing the twenty-six County Republic into the concept of Ireland, as it suggested that the national project in the South was somehow complete, while for them it plainly was not.

The concept of the 'island of Ireland' offered a means of addressing North–South issues without directly or explicitly questioning jurisdictional divisions. In 1988, for instance, the Commission used the concept to highlight the need for community initiatives at the all-Ireland level in the 1989–93 framework for the expenditure of EU structural funds. The term 'island' had a common sense appeal that was virtually irresistible, even to those whose primary political purpose was to preserve Northern Ireland's link with Britain. By the 1990s, it was being used by the British government (notably in the Downing Street Declaration) and by unionist and loyalist politicians.

It was no accident that this shift in EU nomenclature coincided with the acceleration of EU integration in the mid to late 1980s, as the SEM and the proposed EMU were defining an EU 'economic space' without internal borders. In Ireland, the new regionalist definitions were founded on a relatively non-contentious geographic concept and provided ideological legitimation for the Commission's North–South policy initiatives and for cooperation between the Republic and state authorities in the North. In this context, a degree of consensus on the question of regional integration in Ireland and in the EU emerged between political parties in both parts of Ireland.

The North

Reflecting sharpened national conflict which continued after EU membership, political divisions between nationalists identifying with Ireland and unionists identifying with Britain, continued to widen in the 1970s. In Northern Ireland, twenty per cent of Protestants saw themselves as 'Irish' in 1968 while twenty per cent of Catholics saw themselves as 'British'; by 1989, the equivalent figures were three per cent and eight per cent. But at the same time, a regionalist redefinition of national identity was underway, heavily influenced by EU integration, with a degree of convergence on definitions of identity which linguistically and symbolically encompassed both identities (Moxon–Browne 1991). The inclusive concept of 'Northern Irish' for instance, became more popular as it could express both an affiliation to definitially separate 'Northern' Ireland at the same time as it expressed an affiliation to Ireland in general.[7]

This paradox of coexistence between inclusive and exclusive affiliations was reflected in political preferences in Northern Ireland. Inclusive, regionalist redefinitions of political identity, for instance, offered the basis for more malleable political categories, particularly for nationalists and republicans.[8] This was a key factor in the emergence of a relative political consensus on the need for power-sharing political institutions in the North, with veto powers for both nationalists and unionists. In a survey conducted by *Initiative '92* in 1993, for instance, eighty-six per cent of Northern Catholics were found to support this option, together with forty-six per cent of Protestants, adding up to sixty-three per cent overall.[9]

This superseding of communal and political boundaries, just as in other respects they were being sharpened, was also a strong theme in public responses to EU integration. The issue of whether Northern Ireland should join the European Union (EU) split both political blocs in Northern Ireland: constitutional nationalists and some 'official' unionists favoured

Table 3.1 PERCENTAGE FAVOURING UK WITHDRAWAL FROM THE EU

	Northern Ireland	United Kingdom
1975 Referendum	47.9	32.8
(turnout)	(47.4)	(64.5)
1991 Eurobarometer poll	5.2	19.3
(survey number)	(300)	(1000)

Source: Derby 1993; Eurobarometer 36, Autumn 1991.

membership while republicans and loyalists opposed it. An opinion poll held in 1978 suggested that this reflected public attitudes to the EU, with roughly half of all Protestants and half of all Catholics favouring continued EU membership (Guelke 1988, p. 157). Furthermore, after EC membership, this cross-community support for integration grew at a remarkable rate. As illustrated in Table 3.1, at the time of the referendum in 1975, Northern Ireland was the most anti-EU of UK regions by 1991, it was the most 'Europhile' region in the UK.

This reflected a strengthened, shared regional identity of Northern Ireland as part of the EU, which both nationalist and unionist politicians could claim to represent. As elsewhere in the EU, this regional consensus was defined against central state authorities, in this case, over issues such as subsidiarity and additionality (Hainsworth, 1992). Politicians competed to define themselves as regional ambassadors, defending regional interests and maximising the flow of EU funds to the region – a type of 'pork barrel regionalism' (Murray, 1992, p. 21). These tendencies emerged in parallel with the on-going national conflict, and often conflicted with its logic–disrupting ideological positions in the conflict, forcing policy realignments along regionalist lines and potentially recasting 'national' constituencies.

Although attitudes to the EU cut across sectarian lines, party political leaderships mobilised for EP elections on traditional nationalist versus unionist lines. Due to what the British government called 'special circumstances' in Northern Ireland, the region was defined as a single Euro-constituency, with its three MEPs selected under the proportional representation system.[10] Partly as a result of this, EP elections were treated as a contest for political leadership in the North and as a vote for or against the dilution of UK sovereignty, and by implication, the dilution of Northern Ireland's constitutional status as part of the UK. Consequently, the sectarian divide has been most clearly drawn in EP elections. There are few transfers across the communal divide and cross-community parties, such as the Alliance and Workers Party, fare worse in European than in either Westminster or local government elections (O'Leary, 1990; Guelke, 1988, p. 156).

This has favoured the DUP which tripled its share of the Northern vote from 10.2 per cent in the 1979 Westminster election to 29.8 per cent in the European election of that year, claiming 170,688 first preference votes – an event described as 'one of the most important years in DUP history'.[11] EP elections also favoured the SDLP, which in 1979 claimed 24.6 per cent of the vote, 4.7 per cent more than in the 1979 Westminster election and 7.1 per cent more than in the 1981 local government elections. In contrast, the UUP, which fielded two candidates in the 1979 election, saw its share fall by 14.7 per cent to 21.9 per cent of the vote.

Although the DUP continued to top the poll after 1979, there was a slight movement away from the anti-Maastricht DUP and Sinn Féin, towards the less anti-EU UUP and, more significantly, towards the pro-EU SDLP. Both the DUP and Sinn Féin saw their share of the vote fall by 3.4 per cent between 1984 and 1994; the less negative UUP saw its vote increase by 2.4 per cent, while SDLP vote rose by 6.8 per cent over the same ten year period (Table 3.2). In effect, voters were favouring political parties with a positive programme for European integration, perhaps reflecting the growing acceptance, even enthusiasm, for European integration from the mid 1980s.

Increasingly, the three Northern Ireland MEPs worked together on what were defined as joint regional concerns (Elliott, 1990). Funding, 'additionality' and representation at the EU level were common themes in election material, reflecting an emerging political consensus on such issues (Hainsworth, 1992, p. 151). The parties were forced to collaborate in 'getting the best deal' for Northern Ireland, cross-party voting on regional issues in the EP was commonplace

Table 3.2 EP ELECTIONS IN NORTHERN IRELAND: PERCENTAGE
OF VOTES CAST

	UUP	DUP	SDLP	SF	Alliance	WP	Other	Turnout
1979	21.9	29.8	24.6	–	6.8	0.8	16.1	57
1984	21.5	33.6	22.1	13.3	5.0	1.3	3.2	65
1989	22.2	29.9	25.5	9.2	5.2	1.0	7.1	44
1994	23.8	29.2	28.9	9.9	4.1	1.0	3.1	49

Source: O'Leary 1990, *Irish Times* 14 June 1994.

and the three MEPs often made joint representations to the Commission and to the British government.

As early as 1980, all three MEPs visited Brussels with the Mayor of Belfast to call for more EU spending in Northern Ireland. In 1981, they complained that the British government was, as the Reverend Paisley put it, 'siphoning off money intended for Ulster into its own coffers' and in 1985 the three MEPs joined with the Ulster Farmers' Union and the NIEC to lobby Brussels for an increased milk quota under the Common Agricultural Policy (CAP).[12] In 1988 MEPs were united in their condemnation of the Northern Ireland Office (NIO) after the proposed 1989–93 Community Support Framework for Northern Ireland attracted fifty per cent per capita less than the Republic's submission. In 1993, they were unified in opposing the criteria used for allocating cohesion funds and jointly met with the British PM on the issue. They returned to Northern Ireland with the promise that the Treasury would top-up Northern Ireland public expenditure levels, as the only 'Objective One' region not to be allocated 'cohesion' money. As the *Irish News* noted, when it came to defining themselves as doing the 'best' for Northern Ireland, 'cash was thicker than blood'.[13]

A measure of the surprise at such joint action and how it conflicted with the politicians' positions in the national conflict can be gauged from news reports in 1988 after a press lunch for the MEPs in the Commission's Belfast offices, where the SDLP's John Hume and the Reverend Paisley sat side by side, stating there was nothing unusual in the two parties agreeing on socio-economic issues. The two MEPs clarified that it was their 'duty' to get the 'best' for Northern Ireland and although no press photographs were permitted, the next day the *Irish Times* announced that 'John and Ian unite in amity'.[14]

Party policies

Partly as a result of ostensibly ad hoc, 'non political' joint action, there was a significant shifting of position in official party policies. In effect, representatives attempted to construct a consistency between their ideological positions in the national conflict and the logic of regional integration in the EU. This was the case across the political spectrum.

Amongst nationalists, the party most influenced by EU integration was the SDLP. Regional integration in the EU was seen as stimulating a reassessment of North–South relations in Ireland. In 1992, for instance, the party leader called for equal treatment of 'Objective One' regions under the 'cohesion fund' and for a North–South economic policy commission to manage the 'integration of the whole Irish economy within the new Europe'.[15] In 1977, at its seventh annual conference, the party had highlighted the socio-economic impacts of EU membership and in 1984 it argued that these constituted an alternative agenda, separate from the sectarian politicking of rival candidates. Ten years later, the 1994 manifesto, *Towards a New Century*, also concentrated on such issues. Under the slogan 'Europe for people and people for Europe, the party emphasised issues such as the CAP, the Social Charter, the European employment initiative and environmental issues, emphasising the influence it could wield as a member of the Socialist Group. In successive EP elections, the party defined itself, and its candidate John Hume, as an expert on EU issues: the party's 1984 manifesto, *Strength in Europe*, spoke of his 'political effort and political expertise . . . as compared with the negative and destructive attitudes of our main opponents'. The party campaigned for continued EU membership in the 1975 referendum and at Westminster supported both the Single European Act (1988) and the Maastricht Treaty (1993).

Sinn Féin shifted closer to the SDLP position, reflecting greater acceptance of the EU dimension to politics in Ireland.

The party programme, *Éire Nua*, published in 1971 had favoured a strong Irish national state that would distance itself from the 'rich men's club of former colonial powers in the EC'. In its first EP election campaign in 1984, the party fought the election primarily on issues directly related to the conflict. Its manifesto, *One Ireland, One People, The Only Alternative*, argued that the EU had 'subjugated' Ireland to the interests of larger EU states and called for a 'negotiated withdrawal', substituting trade agreements for EU membership. At the same time the party campaigned for 'the maximum benefits available', demanding improved levels of grant aid and suggesting that EU advice centres should be set up in farming communities. The 1989 manifesto, *For a Free Ireland in a Free Europe*, argued that Europeanism was no replacement for Irishness and again called for the renegotiation of Ireland's EU membership. Consistent with this position, in 1992, it published *Democracy or Dependency – The Case Against Maastricht* and campaigned for a 'no' vote during the Maastricht Treaty referendum in the Republic.

But by 1991, Sinn Féin leader was admitting that the party's 'inability to latch onto the European dimension is a source of frustration for me'.[16] With the 1994 manifesto, *Peace in Ireland, a European Issue*, there was a substantial shift as the party moved from outright condemnation of the EU, to arguing that it was possible to construct 'an alternative to the unde-mocratic, anti-worker EU'. EU policies were still seen as the product of imperialist ideology, aimed at the 'creation of an economic and political superpower', servicing the needs of transnational corporations and international finance rather than the 'interests of the actual people of the community'. Similarly, the Maastricht Treaty was criticised not simply for the 'democratic deficit' but also because it would 'erode further the power and sovereignty of EU member states'. But EU integration was not therefore rejected. On the contrary, it was seen as a key site of political engagement and the party came close to praising the EU for its use of funds 'to promote the image of "the island of Ireland" as one unified economy', regretting that this was not expressed in the policy priorities of either the Republic or Northern Ireland.

Other non-unionist parties also moved towards accepting the logic of EU regional integration in Ireland. The Workers'

Party, political descendants of the 'official' IRA, was opposed to EU membership in 1972. However by 1989, it had become more positive about EU developments and the possibilities for political intervention to improve Northern Ireland's position within it. To this end, the party argued for improved representation for Northern Ireland at the EU level and saw the EU framework as a means of superseding the 'medieval quagmire' of sectarianism in Northern Ireland.[17] It fought the 1994 EP election on socio-economic issues, especially employment and poverty, standing candidates in three Irish constituencies – in the North, in Dublin and Munster. Its manifesto, *Peace, Work, Democracy, Class Politics*, highlighted the need to construct 'Left unity' at the EU level in order to challenge the EU's neo-liberal policy agendas, which had left 400,000 unemployed in Ireland, North and South. In Northern Ireland the party called for a boost in EU regional funds, at least to £3 billion sterling, in proportion with the Republic and called for consideration of an Antrim–Scotland road link. On constitutional issues, it urged active EU intervention through an update of the 'Haagerrup Report' – the EP's 1984 investigation into politics in Northern Ireland (see Chapter Four).

Unionists were generally opposed to EU integration as it was seen as diminishing the significance of British sovereignty and, by implication, undermining North–South divisions in Ireland. Ironically though, the smaller parties associated with loyalist paramilitaries were amongst the least hostile to EU integration. Consistent with a preference for Northern Ireland independence, there was general acceptance of the need for North–South economic linkages, but only as a 'working partnership between two states', suggesting, in 1993, that 'the two parts of Ireland are far too small to paddle with their own canoes'.[18]

Of the 'mainstream' unionist parties, only the small cross-community 'Alliance' party defined itself as pro-EU. It endorsed regionalisation as a means of overcoming divisions in Northern Ireland and in its 1989 manifesto, *Show Europe a New Face*, argued for coordinated EU action on regional development in Ireland. The 1994 manifesto, *Our Future Together in Europe*, called for regional government in Northern Ireland to improve representation at the EU level and to 'provide . . . a political structure which all sections of this community could support'.

The party favoured accelerated EU integration and its candidate, Mary Clark-Glass, concentrated on socio-economic, environmental and international issues rather than on Northern Ireland constitutional issues.

Unlike the Alliance, the UUP was ideologically opposed to the concept of European regionalism but nonetheless became relatively positive on some issues of integration in the 1980s. In the 1975 referendum, the party was undecided, primarily because of the pro-European, pro-CAP rural vote. Some politicians favoured membership while others, including Jim Molyneaux, argued that European integration undermined Northern Ireland's constitutional position in the UK.[19]

In its 1989 manifesto, *Europe in the '90s*, the party welcomed EU trade policies, arguing that 'the lifting of trade barriers will increase cross-border trade within the island of Ireland' and emphasised that it had 'campaigned hard to have the present Éire restrictions on cross-border trade removed'. In a section on 'relations with the Republic of Ireland', the party clarified that it was 'not opposed to cooperation where there are no political or constitutional implications'. These issues did not deserve a mention in the 1994 manifesto, *Europe: Making it Work for Ulster*, perhaps suggesting that they had become politically sensitive. The manifesto returned to more general assertions of the need for Northern Ireland to be placed on an equal footing with its European partners and discussed the role of their candidate in promoting a 'two-way awareness' and helping 'to win new understanding of the Province's difficulties'.

Nonetheless, the party, particularly its more 'liberal' wing, had begun to recognise the necessity for North–South links. Speaking in Cork in 1993, Ken Maginnis (UUP MP) called for both parts of Ireland to develop and exploit common strengths, emphasising that the Republic needed to adopt more facilitative and less combative relations with the North.[20] In addition, amongst some UUP border councillors, there was increased acceptance of an EU-induced reduction in the significance of the border.[21] This was also reflected in the McGimpsey brothers' submission to the Opsahl Commission (one of whom was a UUP councillor in the Shankill area and an honorary UUP secretary). This favoured strengthened North–South linkages between the two administrations to allow a 'questioning of old notions of nationalism' in the South as well as to 'achieve social and economic benefit for the Irish people as a whole'.[22]

The party also addressed the issue of North–South relations in its position paper, *Blueprint for Stability*, of February 1994, in which the approach outlined in 1989 was deepened, suggesting a closer engagement with and acceptance of EU-related issues. On North–South constitutional issues, arguments for the removal of Articles two and three of the Republic's Constitution were phrased in terms of the need to learn from 'European cooperation, namely recognition of existing frontiers, abandonment of territorial ambition and mutual cooperation in an atmosphere of respect for human rights'. The party emphasised that it was its 'ambition . . . to develop cooperation on matters of mutual interest and concern' with the Republic. Supporting this, there was acceptance of the need to incorporate the European Convention on Human Rights and Conference on Security and Cooperation in Europe (CSCE) declarations on minority rights into the Northern Ireland legal system.[23]

The DUP was more actively hostile to EU integration. It campaigned against membership in 1975 and in 1979 saw itself as participating in the EP to maximise EU transfers to Northern Ireland and to put the loyalist case at the European level. In 1984, the party stressed issues such as additionality and the need for more regional funding and argued that their candidate, as an independent, was concerned 'only with advancing the cause of Northern Ireland'. There were similar themes in the 1989 manifesto, with a particular stress on the party's independence as 'a free and unfettered voice' in the EP. In 1992, the party was 'implacably opposed' to the Maastricht Treaty, yet was committed to maximising inflows of EU funds – to 'milking the cow before slitting its throat'.[24] These themes were confirmed in 1994 when the candidate claimed he had 'no ties with any group which is pro-EC and anti-Ulster in character', clarifying that 'we oppose the creation of a European super-state or anything which strikes at the sovereignty of the UK'.

This was set against the party's substantial commitment to EU structures and to coordinated EU action in support of 'national' policies. By 1994, these went well beyond 'milking' the EU cow. In 1992, the party had begun to argue for 'cooperation in Europe without incorporation', a position similar to that of the UUP.[25] By 1994, it was calling for EU action on unemployment, proposing a new commissioner to 'channel the resources of the community into reducing unemployment'. Similarly, it welcomed the creation of a commissioner for consumer affairs. It favoured EU action on working conditions, supporting the EU Social Charter, and called for the creation of an EU inspectorate to enforce regulations on the transportation of live animals. On other issues, EU conditions were used as a yardstick, for instance, in developing a 'family policy' under which an income would be provided for 'fulltime mothers equivalent at least to the minimum wage in many EC states'.

Overall, then, there was some convergence between political parties in Northern Ireland on issues of EU integration. Parties initially opposed to EU membership participated in this consensus-forming process, suggesting that EU integration had created a framework for political conflict along regionalist, rather than nationalist, lines. This was mirrored by developments in the Republic.

The South

In the Republic, political debate on the process of EU integration also focused increasingly on the content of integration rather than the question of integration itself. Public enthusiasm for the EU had traditionally been high in the Republic. In May 1972, eighty-three per cent of voters approved the proposal to join the EU, after a campaign in which the two major political parties, Fianna Fáil and Fine Gael, along with the political establishment in the Senate and the Department of Foreign Affairs, wholeheartedly supported membership.[26] Voter enthusiasm for EU integration was also reflected in the referenda which approved the 1987 Single European Act (SEA) and the 1993 Maastricht Treaty and in successive Eurobarometer polls. In 1991 for instance, 5.3 per cent favoured withdrawal from the EU, compared with 7.2 per cent in the Community as a whole (*Eurobarometer 36*, Autumn 1991). In 1992, 70.2 per cent saw the EU as a 'good thing', comparing with 46.5 per cent in

Table 3.3 EUROPEAN PARLIAMENT ELECTIONS IN THE REPUBLIC:
PERCENTAGE OF VOTES

	FF	FG	LP	SF	PD	WP	Green	Ind	(turnout)
1979	34.7	33.1	14.5	–	–	3.3		14.1	(63.6)
1984	39.2	32.2	8.4	4.9	–	4.3	0.5	10.1	(47.6)
1989	31.5	21.6	9.5	2.3	11.9	7.5	3.8	11.9	(68.3)
1994	35.0	24.3	11.0	3.0	6.5	6.5	3.7	6.9	(37.0)

Source: EP (1989) EP elections 1989: results and elected members, PE 133.339, 22
June 1989; *Financial Times*, 14 June 1994.

Northern Ireland, 43.1 per cent in the UK and 60.4 per cent in
the EU as a whole.[27]

Arguably this pro-Europeanism was reflected in voting
patterns (see Table 3.3). As the range of pro-EU political parties
widened, there was a movement of votes away from the main,
largely pro-EU parties, Fine Gael and Fianna Fáil. In 1979,
these two parties jointly accounted for 67.8 per cent of the vote
and nine seats, rising to 71.4 per cent of the vote in 1984 and
fourteen seats. By 1989 however, their proportion of votes cast
fell to 52.7 per cent, with ten seats. In 1994, partly due to the
low turnout, their vote rose to 69.3 per cent, but only increased
their representation by one seat, contrasting with the Irish
Green Party which gained its first two seats in the EP.

While this could have reflected a general disillusionment
with the two main political parties, it also, at least in part,
reflected a move towards greater political engagement with
EU related issues by a wider range of political parties. As in
Northern Ireland, this was reflected in party policies.

Party policies

During the 1972 membership referendum, the EU was presented as a useful forum for the pursuit of the Republic's
specific interests, particularly in agriculture. Only on the Left
was there opposition to membership – in the trade union
movement and in the Irish Labour Party, the Green Party, the
Irish Communist Party and in 'official' Sinn Féin (later the
Workers' Party and the Democratic Left). This was largely due

to its expected impact on the Republic's military neutrality and its likely damage to industry. Nonetheless, as in Northern Ireland, these parties later became less implacably opposed to EU integration.

The most pro-EU party, Fine Gael, was dedicated to the development of the EU as a 'moral enterprise' (Ruane and Todd, 1992a). It was fully committed in its party constitution to working towards a united Europe and defined itself, in the European People's Party, as within the mainstream of European Christian Democracy. At the same time, it was committed to protecting the powers and interests of Irish state representatives as a condition of increased integration. When in government, the party opposed diminution in the Commission's 'exclusive power of initiative', which was seen as the key to preventing the domination of EU institutions by the larger member states.[28] Consequently, the party's 1994 EP manifesto, *Working for Ireland at the Heart of Europe*, called for a 'democratic constitution for a strong EU' while at the same time opposing 'any proposal which is designed to create differential membership terms or status for larger states in the Union'.

Fianna Fáil was more sceptical of integration. In 1985–6 it called for a renegotiation of the SEA, in alliance with the French Gaullists in the European Democratic Alliance. The following year, this opposition was reversed and the party fully endorsed the Act in the 1987 referendum. By the 1990s, the party supported the transition to European Union: in 1991 its leader, Charles Haughey, participated as Taoiseach in the inter-governmental conference which approved the Maastricht Treaty in 1991, and in 1992 the party campaigned for a 'yes' vote in the Maastricht Treaty referendum. Reflecting this shift, in 1990 the party adopted a more positive position on the role of the EU in the national conflict, calling on the Commission to address the 'totality of relations between all parties of these islands' (Ruane and Todd, 1992a).[29]

The shift in Irish Labour Party policy came later. The party campaigned against the SEA in 1987, but by 1989, with its manifesto *Towards 1992*, it had adopted a pro-integration position and argued for a strengthened regional and social dimension to EU policies. By the 1992 referendum, it was advocating critical endorsement of the Maastricht Treaty, stressing the dangers of EU deregulation for employment and social development in the Republic.[30] In 1994, it campaigned in favour of EU integration as part of the move to a united socialist Europe. Its manifesto, *Europe for the People*, was positive about the process of EU integration and stressed that it was only through 'cooperation and coherent policies' at the EU level that issues of employment, social development and environmental protection could be addressed.

Similarly, by 1994 the Workers' Party was supporting EU integration. Two years earlier it had called for a 'no' vote in the Maastricht Treaty, to allow a renegotiation to safeguard Irish neutrality and to protect the Republic's economy from the EMU 'convergence criteria'.[31] This was mirrored in policy positions adopted by the Democratic Left, which split from the Workers Party' in 1992. Its 1994 manifesto, *Towards a Democratic Europe*, for instance, focused on attempting to shift the political agenda at the EU level away from neo-liberalism, towards an eco-socialist agenda, for a 'people's Europe built on cooperation rather than competition'. Finally, in 1994 the Irish Green Party also became more actively engaged with political issues at the EU level. It opposed the Maastricht Treaty in 1992, but two years later its manifesto, *Guarantee the Earth*, presented a detailed agenda for environmental improvements, all to be implemented at the EU level.

Overall, concerns about loss of sovereignty for the Republic in the EU were replaced by concerns about the content of EU policies. Party political positions on the issue of EU integration appeared to converge, as left–right inter-party conflict between the parties was translated or transposed to the EU level.

North and South

Given these shifts in party policy, to some degree reflected in voting patterns, there are grounds for arguing that the process of EU integration was leading to a degree of convergence, North and South, towards a shared acceptance of the process of EU integration and towards a common policy agenda on EU related issues. The EU had effectively become a fact of political life in both jurisdictions, leading to significant revisions in party policies, even on issues relating to national sovereignty.

As early as 1972, Garret Fitzgerald, who was later to become leader of Fine Gael, predicted that many of the 'reserved powers' that were retained by Westminster under the 1920 Government of Ireland Act were likely to be exercised at the EU rather than at the UK level (Fitzgerald, 1972, p. 109). These included foreign affairs, external defence, nationality, corporation and income tax, customs and excise duties, trade marks and patents, external trade and currency regulation, all of which, after the Maastricht Treaty, were at least partially exercised at the EU level. Politicians in Ireland, North and South, had begun to compete in defining the agenda for these issues at the EU level. To a degree, this shifted ideological conflict out of the 'national' state framework and into a supra-state EU regional framework.

This assessment perhaps over-emphasises these region-alising impacts, and plays down on-going ideological conflict over sovereignty related issues. Indeed, the one remaining 'reserved' power under the 1920 Act cited by Fitzgerald in 1972, namely the absolute power of the 'Crown in Parliament', remained central to the concept of state sovereignty in the UK and was at least as symbolically important to political affiliations in Northern Ireland as it was prior to EU membership in 1972. Regardless of the explicitly political dimensions of EU integration, for instance on citizenship rights, these claims to sovereignty in Northern Ireland remained firmly in place, in practical as well as in symbolic terms (Boyle and Hadden, 1994, p. 146). These issues of on-going and perhaps sharpened nationalist divergence in Ireland are examined in the next sub-section.

3.2 DIVERGING NATIONALISMS

The two Irish economies are among the most open and dependent economies in the EU but, in many respects, political configurations in the Republic as well as in Northern Ireland are still defined by ideological conflict over the 'national' question (O'Donnell, 1993a, p. 40). Indeed, the '1992' changes, leading to greater cross-border collaboration in financial, economic and social relations, 'merely serve(d) to highlight the extent to which the continuing existence of the border was determined by political and cultural forces' (Hickman, 1990, p. 21).

All the major political parties, North and South, with the exception of the South's Labour Party, were born out of national conflict and very few bridge the border. Only the Workers' Party, Sinn Féin and the Communist Party stood candidates on an all-Ireland basis in the 1970s and 1980s. Furthermore, political movements are also divided between northern and southern elements: there are separate civil liberties organisations for North and South; environmental campaigns are centred on either of the two jurisdictions, rarely both; voluntary and community development agencies such as 'Combat Poverty' and the 'Community Development Workers' Cooperative' are focused exclusively on the South, while the Northern Ireland Council for Voluntary Action is focused on the North; the pro-choice campaign in favour of decriminalising abortion in the North was organised separately from its Southern counterpart, reflecting divisions in the women's movement which had only intermittently been organised on an island-wide basis (Ward, 1991).

There are separate business organisations, commercial groupings and agricultural associations for North and South, invariably articulating their particular rather than common interests. Cultural organisations are also divided between North and South – even most Irish language agencies are separately organised. While the major religious organisations, such as the Protestant Church of Ireland, the Presbyterian Church and the Catholic Church, are organised on an all-island basis, the Protestant Churches rarely articulate their concerns in an all-Ireland framework. The same is true of the trade union movement, which is organised on an all-Ireland basis through the Irish Congress of Trade Unions, but has only recently been engaged in linking the concerns of Northern and Southern workers (since the mid 1980s). The sporting world has also retained all-Ireland structures but again, unevenly, for rugby, boxing and Gaelic sports, but crucially, not for soccer.

While formal politics is almost fully partitioned, significant aspects of economic and cultural life remain organised on an all-Ireland, cross-border basis, reflecting the uneven historical legacy of national conflict. But this cross-border 'permeability' is rarely, if ever, politicised, as to do so would be to immediately undermine the 'positive sum' basis on which such linkages are maintained (Whyte, 1983, 1991). Hence the weakness of North–South organisations reflects 'zero-sum' conflicts between unionism and nationalism, in which Irish nationalists are seen as pursuing an aspiration that, if successful, directly diminishes the rights of British nationalists and Ulster Unionists: if the Republic gains a greater role in political affairs in the North then, as the unionist Cadogan Group has argued, 'Unionists give up something real and tangible and they give it up for good'.[32]

These conflicting fears and hopes were reflected in opinions on the impact of the removal of borders in the EU. While the SDLP stressed the 'magnetic' force driving border communities together in the context of the EU, the UUP emphasised that the border divided two 'nations', expressing, as John Taylor the UUP MP and former MEP called it, 'the fundamental division between the two races that live on this island'.[33] This was translated into open hostility towards the concept of a 'borderless' EU with repeated calls to 'seal' the border, from UUP as well as DUP politicians.[34] Hence, the political response to EU integration, in the Republic as well as in Northern Ireland, was heavily influenced by the national conflict. In what follows, these influences are examined in some detail, again primarily using party policy documents and European election manifestos.

The North

The political logic of the national conflict was reflected in the electoral framework for the EP elections in Northern Ireland. As noted earlier, the region was defined as one constituency and the elections are run under the Single Transferable Vote (STV) system, as in the Republic, although the vote is held on the same day as in Britain. The use of the STV system and the allocation of three seats for Northern Ireland, two more than the UK government initially intended on the basis of relative population, reflected a desire to ensure that Northern nationalists obtained at least one representative in the EP (Elliott,

1980). The Commission and the Republic had pressed for these concessions which were agreed by the UK government on condition that it received an increased allocation of seats overall (Fitzgerald, 1991). As noted earlier, this helped to ensure that the national divide in Northern Ireland was more clearly defined in European elections than in elections for Westminster or for local authorities. As a result, in terms of electioneering, issues in the national conflict rather than specifically EU issues have tended to shape the political agenda. These have been increasingly intermingled with EU themes, begging the question of whether the national conflict is being Europeanised or whether the European dimension is being sectarianised (Arthur, 1985).

The SDLP, the most Europhile of all the main parties in Ireland, substantially recast its nationalist agenda in the EU context. In 1982, the party appealed to the EP to 'grasp the nettle' in Northern Ireland as the conflict was an 'affront to community ideals', and in its 1984 election manifesto, the party viewed the Parliament as a platform for airing Northern Ireland's grievances.[35] It argued that the debate around the Haagerrup report, which John Hume had initiated through the Socialist Group of the EP, was the 'first international debate' on the North's problems and that the Parliament had offered a forum to focus international attention on human rights abuses in Northern Ireland (the report is discussed in Chapter Four). In addition, it argued that European integration necessitated action at the all-Ireland level: it complained about the British failure to present Northern Ireland's case and suggested agricultural support should be distributed at an all-Ireland level, to reflect shared interests of North and South.

Ten years later, in the 1994 EP elections, the party had developed these campaigning themes into a position that expressed the nationalist aspiration to greater unity in Ireland within a wider 'Europe of the Regions'. The election address spoke of the 'the ever closer union of the peoples of Europe [and] the breaking down of old conflicts and barriers' as a 'major source of assistance in tackling our own problems'. The manifesto avoided any detailed discussion of what this implied for the North, partly reflecting unionist accusations that the SDLP was imposing its nationalist views on the EU integration process. The only – oblique – reference to Northern Ireland's relationship with Britain was the argument that 'there must be effective direct representation of Northern Ireland in Europe, and joint approaches with the Republic, if we are to maximise the advantages of EU membership'.[36]

Clearer indications that the party was developing a regionalist agenda emerged in party statements from the early 1980s. In 1988, the party leader argued that the SEM would lead to 'harmonisation of both parts of Ireland', arguing that 'many of the divisions will have to go'.[37] Two years later, in 1990, he brought a piece of concrete from Belfast's 'peace line' to a European Socialist conference in Berlin, to demonstrate his belief in the 'powerful example that Europe provides for Northern Ireland'. In the same year at the SDLP conference, he claimed that 'sovereignty and independence are no longer Northern issues', and that this made it 'much easier to accommodate both [nationalist and unionist] identities'.[38] Later, in a speech to a Church of Ireland congregation in Belfast, unionists were offered a role in the 'ever closer [European] union between Britain and Ireland and North and South in Ireland'.[39]

More detailed implications were mapped out in party policy papers. The 1992 position paper, *The SDLP Analysis of the Nature of the Problem*, argued that 'pooling of sovereignty' in the EU would enable people to 'work their common ground together at their own speeds towards a unity that respects diversity', founded on substate regionalisation and democratic EU institutions, which the party leader described as a 'dilation of democracy'.[40] This had clear implications for North–South issues. In its 1988 policy statement, *1992: The Implications of the Single Market for Northern Ireland*, the party had argued that, '1992 will mean the effective disappearance of the border for practical and commercial purposes' and in 1990 the party leader suggested that with the onset of European Union, the North–South border would become little more than a 'county boundary'.[41]

Consequently, in its submission to the NIO on the 1994–99 EU funding round, the SDLP argued that there should be the 'maximum integration possible' and greater coordination of government plans in every aspect of EU expenditure. It was suggested that cross-border authorities with tax-raising powers in both state jurisdictions should be created in partnership with the European Commission, to manage the separate INTERREG fund for border regions.[42] On more directly constitutional issues, the party was willing to encourage arrangements that would allow the two communities 'to share the island short of a single island state' and in 1992, it presented specific proposals, modelled on EU institutions, to 'strand one' of the Brooke talks. A six member 'Commission' for Northern Ireland was favoured, composed of three representatives from the North, elected under the STV system (effectively UUP, DUP and SDLP), a representative for each of the two governments and a European Commission representative acting as neutral arbiter, making the proposals a 'bit easier for other people [i.e. – unionists] to accept'.[43] The Commission would exercise executive powers in tandem with a North–South Parliamentary Assembly and an Anglo–Irish intergovernmental body, mirroring institutional arrangements at the EU level.[44]

To a degree, this increasing articulation of nationalist aspirations in a regionalist, EU framework shifted the framework for ideological conflict in Northern Ireland, forcing Unionists to abandon rejectionism and to compete with the SDLP to define themselves as the more capable 'ambassadors' at the EU level. This was no less true of the Republican movement which also built closer ideological linkages between its position in the national conflict and its interpretation of EU integration.

When it first stood candidates in an EP election in 1984, Sinn Féin campaigned primarily on issues related to the conflict, arguing that a Sinn Féin victory would undermine British authority and force the Dublin government into a fundamental reappraisal of its 'disastrous, grovelling stance on the North'. By 1992, the focus had shifted to the EU: in its policy document, *Towards a Lasting Peace*, the party argued that there was a considerable stock of goodwill in favour of Irish unification at the EU level and proposed that the Dublin government should make greater use of this in pursuit of 'national reconciliation' in Ireland.

In 1992, the party leader appealed for an EU human rights monitoring group to be established in Northern Ireland, and at the party's Ard Fheis he argued that 'the involvement of the British government in Ireland is a European issue'.[45] In 1993, Sinn Féin representatives visited the European Commission and the Belgian Presidency in Brussels, calling for an enhanced EU role in the conflict. The following year the party announced it would be setting up an office in Brussels, 'heralding a change in the party's approach to the EU'.[46]

The party became convinced that EU integration changed Britain's reasons for remaining in Ireland, and that it encouraged North–South integration.[47] Concepts of all-Ireland democratic economic management encouraged by the EU formed a central theme in the Sinn Féin *Submission to Initiative '92*, of November 1992, and were detailed in its policy document, *The Economics of a United Ireland*. Published in February 1994, this argued that 'a united economy could increase wealth creation but without economic democracy it will create less wealth in fewer hands'. The party's 1994 EP manifesto developed this theme further, with the party arguing that without democratic North–South institutions, EU integration would create an 'undemocratic island economy'.

Hence, both Sinn Féin and the SDLP were beginning to fuse their aspiration to Irish unity with a positive aspiration to EU integration. In contrast, unionist politicians were vocal in their condemnation of 'interference' by EU institutions in the affairs of Northern Ireland, especially on North–South issues.

Throughout the 1980s, unionist MEPs were active in complaining about the implications of EU policies for British sovereignty in Northern Ireland, and pressed the European Commission to fund linkages between Northern Ireland and Britain rather than with the Republic. Any move towards a European framework was interpreted by definition, as a move away from UK sovereignty, and by implication, towards an Irish framework for political authority in Northern Ireland in which unionists would be in the minority. EU integration was seen as 'blurring the edges' of the union, muddying the otherwise clear waters of British sovereignty in Northern Ireland. Attempts at shifting the negotiating framework from a 'purely Northern Ireland focus' to a wider perspective of the island as a whole or of 'the totality of relationships within these islands' were seen as contributing to this 'muddying' process and at worst 'confused or devious'.[48]

As with the SDLP and Sinn Féin, the two main unionist parties competed in linking their positions in the national conflict to the process of EU integration. The UUP saw itself as presenting a positive vision of the EU as an inter-state body serving joint interests and preserving individual national sovereignties. The party's manifesto in the 1989 EP election praised the Thatcher government for having 'aligned itself with Unionists' in her 1988 Bruges speech. It asserted that the EU was threatening 'the sovereignty of our nation' and promised that the UUP candidate would be 'safeguarding the integrity of the UK'. Underlining this, its 1990 policy document, *Signposts to the Future*, committed the party to oppose any attempts to 'further erode the role of our national parliament at Westminster'.

The party combined this hesitant pro-Europeanism with its own agenda in the national conflict. In 1993, the party's support for the Maastricht Treaty bought greater Conservative backing for the UUP integrationist agenda. The resulting end to legislation by 'Orders in Council' and the creation of a Select Committee for Northern Ireland at Westminster were stressed by the UUP leader in the party's 1994 campaign material, while emphasising their ability to 'develop contacts and friends for the unionist cause' at the EU level.

On policy issues the party argued for infrastructural investment that would build closer links to Britain, and it opposed improved linkages with the South. In 1981 for instance, Ulster Unionists on the Fermanagh Council opposed cross-border projects regardless of their benefits for the border economy. But later, very similar initiatives were largely accepted under the first spending round for the EU's cross-border INTERREG fund in 1990–3. At the same time, the party demanded that the North should be funded at the same level as the Republic under the Cohesion Fund, calculating that during 1994–9 the EU would be providing £1,960 per head in the South, while the North stood to receive only £760 per head. Despite these ad hoc policy shifts, Ulster Unionists remained particularly vocal in condemning what they saw as a 'takeover' of Northern industry by Southern interests. In 1991, John Taylor (UUP MP) condemned the acquisition of the Northern Trustees Savings Bank by the Allied Irish Bank; in 1992, Ken Maginnis (UUP MP) complained when the Department of the Environment awarded a road building contract to a Southern company; and

in 1993 the UUP MEP, Jim Nicholson, condemned the acquisition of Northern dairy producers by the Southern-owned
Golden Vale.[49]

Some party representatives argued that EU integration
would effectively restore the pre-1921 Union, bringing Ireland
'back under the predominant influence of the British Isles
from which it had been separated for only seventy years'.[50]
This approach was formulated into a proposal for a 'Council
of the British Isles', presented by the party leader at the UUP's
1992 conference. Later in the same year it was tabled as the
party's favoured approach for 'strands two and three' of the
inter-party talks initiated by the Secretary of State, Peter
Brooke. It was envisaged that the Council would provide an
overarching framework within which to manage Anglo–Irish
and North–South relations through, respectively, a British–Irish
Parliamentary body and an Inter-Irish Relations Committee. The
Inter-Irish Committee would allow Southern representatives
from the Dáil to consult with representatives from a Northern
Assembly on a wide range of issues (with executive decisions
reserved for the Assembly and for the Dáil). Such arrangements
would have been unworkable without Northern devolution and
were made conditional on amendment of the Articles two and
three of the Republic's Constitution. The proposals were
rejected by the SDLP as they were seen as excessively
minimalist (allowing the DUP to accuse the UUP of naïvety).
Despite this, they were further elaborated in 1993, although
they were made more firmly conditional on agreement to
remove, not simply to amend, Articles two and three.[51]

The DUP, meanwhile, saw the EU as eroding national
sovereignty and thereby undermining the border. Ian Paisley
joined the EP as a 'free and fearless Protestant and loyalist
voice' and he was the first MEP to speak in the chamber in
1979, to complain that the British flag was upside-down on its
flagpole outside the EP building. Constitutional concerns were
combined with a sectarian branding of the EU as a 'Catholic
institution': in 1984, the party argued that Northern Ireland
was 'the last bastion of Protestantism in Europe and stands
between the Vatican and her goal of a united Roman Catholic
state of Europe'; in 1988, the Reverend Paisley attempted to
disrupt the Papal address during an EP session, culminating

in his being ordered out of the chamber; and in 1992, in an interview, the Reverend William McCrea, DUP MP, looked forward to 'the fall of the system, yes the EC and the fall of Romanism – read the 17th chapter of the Book of Revelations. You get a wonderful view of the fall of Babylon'.[52]

The party fought the 1984 election with the slogan 'the EC puts your pound in Dublin's pocket' and argued that a vote for the DUP was the best way of opposing 'schemes which would ultimately lead to a united Ireland', clarifying that it was 'opposed not merely to our terms of membership but to the very principle of membership itself'. This was tempered somewhat by the need to participate in the EP to counter those 'intent on Ulster's destruction' and to 'milk' the funding régimes, although this was set in the context of religious metaphor and missionary calling – given that the 'Roman Catholic nations' had come together in the EU, the DUP was duty-bound to attend EP sessions, just as 'Daniel, against his will, found himself in Babylon and raised a faithful and fearless voice there'. The party treated the 1989 election as a vote against Tom King, the Secretary of State responsible for the AIA, and the 1994 election was treated as a 'crusade' against the Downing Street Declaration. The party condemned the 'betrayal' of 'giving to Dublin joint authority in shaping the future of Ulster' and labelled the UUP leader as a traitor and a 'Judas' to the Protestant cause for supporting the 1993 Anglo–Irish Declaration, and for agreeing to the creation of North–South institutions. Nonetheless, the party had itself adopted a very similar position to the UUP in its policy paper, *Breaking the Logjam*, in which it had also favoured a new North–South rapprochement and possibly the creation of North–South bodies once Articles two and three had been removed.[53]

Parties linked to loyalist paramilitaries, such as the Ulster Democratic Party, the Ulster Independence Movement and the Third Way/Ulster Nation, campaigned for an independent Northern Ireland, at least for the 'loyal' parts of Northern Ireland, within the EU. Like the UUP, in countering the SDLP demand for a Council of Ireland, the UDA called for a Council of the British Isles. These proposals were overshadowed by its *Planning for Doomsday* document, released early in 1994, in which it called for re-Partition as a last resort for Loyalists, with expulsion, internment or 'nullification' of Catholics remaining in the now fully 'loyal' Northern Ireland.[54]

The Conservative Party in Northern Ireland also treated the 1994 election as a referendum on the national question. Contesting its first EP elections, the party committed itself to defending 'Northern Ireland's position as an integral part of the UK, not just as a region of the EU' and argued that by virtue of its influence in the UK, it would be more able to defend 'Ulster's' interests than its unionist rivals.

In general, unionists tended to see the EU as a 'Trojan horse' (Hainsworth and Morrow, 1993, p. 10). There was an assumed monolithic unity of British sovereignty which in a sense could be punctured by the creation of EU institutions, exercising sovereign powers in tandem with other states, including the Republic. There were widespread fears of the impact of EU integration on Northern Ireland's constitutional status, not unlike fears that emerged during the period of rapprochement between North and South in the mid 1960s. This raises the question of whether nationalist aspirations and unionist fears were correct – whether in fact unionism would be fatally damaged 'without the traditional estrangement from Dublin' (Lyne, 1990, p. 432). Liberal unionist politicians in the 1960s clearly did not think so, to their cost, leading to the emergence of the DUP and the collapse of Stormont.

Overall, as Northern Ireland politicians attempted to construct a consistency between their positions in the national conflict and the process of EU integration, there was a marked degree of political divergence, jarring with the emergence of a limited regionalist consensus. There were similar developments in the Republic.

The South

Since the reunification of Germany, the Republic is the only member of the EU which makes a formal claim to the territory of another member state, through Articles two and three of its 1937 Constitution. This claim is a 'touchstone issue in Irish politics', both in the South and in the North (O'Cleireacain, 1983, p. 108). The state in the Republic was founded on the gains won by Irish nationalists and republicans. Hence repudiation of the aspiration to Irish unity was simply 'not a viable option for a state that is grounded in the legitimacy of Irish Nationalism' (Guelke, 1988, p. 198). As clarified by the Supreme Court in 1975, and again in 1990, politicians in the Republic are obliged to work for Irish unity, but (as discussed in Chapter Four), this was rarely reflected in state policy, although politicians in the Republic displayed a substantial rhetorical commitment to nationalist aspirations.

This was reflected in public attitudes to Irish unity. While there was a strong tendency to equate the twenty-six county state with 'Ireland', there was a firm, and recently growing, commitment to Irish unity. This led to a paradoxical growth in 'national' aspirations alongside a growth in 'regional' consciousness. As the *Irish Times* pointed out, 'most people in the Republic live in hope of unity', and were reluctant to remove the Republic's constitutional claim on the North.[55] In 1990, a majority (fifty-three per cent) was in favour of changing Articles two and three, in 1991 this had fallen to forty-eight per cent, in 1992 to forty per cent and in 1993 to thirty-nine per cent.[56] As outlined in Table 3.4, aspirations to unity rose in the 1980s, as did expectations of unity in the coming twenty-five to fifty years. In a poll conducted by Maynooth College in 1992 on the question of political structures, the vast majority in the Republic favoured the creation of a single all-Ireland government, seventy-five per cent viewing it as 'desirable'.[57]

However, when it came to practical politics as opposed to aspirations and hopes, there was little commitment to achieving unity. People in the Republic may have had an emotional attachment to unity but were content to keep it as a remote possibility.[58] In particular, peace in the North and prosperity in the South were more important than Irish unity: in 1991, eighty-two per cent in the South were willing to postpone Irish unity to allow a peaceful settlement in Northern Ireland, and in 1993, seventy-five per cent opposed tax rises in the Republic as a possible price for unity.[59] Northern Ireland was seen as a peripheral issue in everyday political life, to the extent that in 1993, when the government was becoming closely involved in the Irish–British dialogue on the North, only one per cent of voters in the Republic considered that the national conflict was a 'major issue'.[60]

Table 3.4 ASPIRATION TO IRISH UNITY IN THE REPUBLIC:
PERCENTAGE OF POLL

| | There will be unity in | | General aspiration to unity |
	25 years	50 years	
1983	39	42	76
1987	49	29	67
1991	30	56	82
1993	39	52	–

Source: *Irish Times*, 22 April and 27 November 1991; *Independent on Sunday*, 12 December 1993.

The combination of nationalist rhetorical commitment to a thirty-two county state and substantive, de facto commitment to furthering the interests of the twenty-six county Irish Republic led to North–South divergence both in terms of cementing the ideological divisions between the Southern nationalist and Northern unionist communities and in terms of the lack of substantive policy initiatives 'on the ground'. As a result, the concept of Irish integration in the context of EU integration proved to be a useful political tool, allowing reliance on non-political socio-economic shifts to deliver political change, thus permitting inaction on issues directly relevant to the conflict.

Irish nationalists had long expected or hoped that EU integration would undermine British sovereignty in the North. Entry into the EU with the UK sat neatly with the reformulation of Irish nationalism in the 1960s – from the agrarian populism of Eamon De Valera, to the 'technocratic anti-partitionism' of Sean Lemass (Lyne, 1990). Politicians in the Republic had a vested interest in preserving domestic tranquillity and in distancing themselves from the Northern issues. Combining the pursuit of Irish integration with the pursuit of EU integration permitted an on-going rhetorical commitment to Irish unity, empty of practical initiatives aimed at 'winning over', or persuading Northern unionists of the merits of all-Ireland unity, either in terms of reform of the Southern state or in terms of building North–South linkages (Arthur, 1985).

111

The formula of relying on EU integration to reduce the 'economic differences that divide North and South', and also to free the South from dependence on Britain, thereby enhancing the self-confidence of politicians in the Republic, was outlined as early as 1962, five years after the Treaty of Rome.[61] When forced to develop a response to the intensifying conflict in Northern Ireland, the Lemass government pursued this agenda, paired with the political conviction, as Liam Cosgrave put it in the Dáil in 1973, that 'reconciliation between its two communities cannot be brought about successfully in isolation from the larger issue of reconciliation within the island as a whole'.[62]

This approach was detailed in the Taoiseach's Statement to the Dáil on the question of EEC membership in March 1972, in which he argued that 'if we were to remain outside the Community, we would be conferring on the border the status of a frontier, both economic and political, between ourselves and the rest of Europe, thereby "copper-fastening" Partition'.[63] Similarly, after the referendum on membership, the Taoiseach, Jack Lynch argued that under the Treaty of Rome, the British government was required to work towards an 'ever closer union of the peoples of Europe' and the British government should take immediate action with the Republic to resolve the Northern conflict.[64] These arguments were repeated during the 1987 referendum in the Republic, when the Minister of Finance in the Republic, Brian Lenihan, argued 'nothing could be more calculated to secure the border' than a vote against the SEA: it would consign the South to 'second grade' EU membership while the North, with Britain, would claim 'first grade' membership.[65] Again, in anticipation of a third referendum on the question of EU integration in 1992, the government argued in its White Paper on the Maastricht Treaty that 'within a closer European Union, the common interests of both parts of Ireland in so many areas of Community activity should become more apparent', helping 'to create closer human links and break down barriers on this island' (DSO, 1992c, p. 32). A vote against European Union was therefore a vote for sharper North–South divisions. Most political parties in the Republic pursued this agenda, combining it with the expectation that EU integration would deperipheralise the

Irish economy – what has been described as a 'conjunction of the interests of the pocket with certain predispositions of the spirit' (Coakley, 1983, p. 64).

Fianna Fáil, with its roots in Irish republicanism, was particularly keen to stress the unifying effects of EU membership. In 1990, Charles Haughey, the Fianna Fáil Taoiseach, saw his personal ideal as 'Irish unity as part of a wider European unity'.[66] At the NIF in 1983, the party leader argued that 'the existence of this artificially sustained economy has prevented the fruitful development of the island as an economic unit'. In 1989, he invited Northern Ireland politicians to come to Dublin to discuss how the Republic could work with the North at the EU level, in the best interests of the island as a whole. (This was followed by his visit to the Northern Institute of Directors conference, discussed above in Chapter Two.)[67] Later, in 1990, at the party's Ard Fheis, he argued that 'the Irish people will be united in a unified Europe' and announced that the Irish Presidency of the EU would be committed to giving special attention to cross-border issues. In an interview with the *Irish Times* Charles Haughey clarified that 'the economies in both parts of Ireland are going to converge as the political, economic and financial barriers between us disappear'. He argued that 'this must have a political fall out', suggesting that 'it is not too romantic to think of a united Ireland as part of a united Europe'.[68] In 1991, these themes were reiterated when he argued, during the Brooke talks, that 'the EC offers us an entirely new context in which to seek political progress in Ireland [that would] soften and eventually eliminate the divisions of the past on this island'.[69]

Partly because of this increased articulation of the party's commitment to Irish integration in tandem with EU integration, in the 1990s Fianna Fáil embarked on a reassessment of its position on Articles two and three. In 1990, it had opposed a proposal to amend the Articles which had the support of Fine Gael, the Workers' Party, the Labour Party and the Progressive Democrats on grounds that the proposal was inopportune rather than on grounds of principle.[70] In 1993, it announced that in the context of a peace settlement, Articles two and three could be amended to express a political aspiration to unity, rather than a legal claim on the North, and the party leader clarified that he was willing to propose an amendment to Article three, making unity conditional upon consent being 'freely given' in the North.[71] This tentative reassessment of the party position on the question of unity was combined with the assumption that EU integration would in some way assist the process of Irish integration. In 1993, for instance, Albert Reynolds argued that the EU would encourage 'development links between the two parts of the island', suggesting that 'in the context of the Single Market there is immense scope and great opportunity for us to work together, North and South, in a more friendly and civilised climate'.[72]

In the early 1990s, the Labour Party leadership also became increasingly enthusiastic about the impact of EU integration on Irish unity. In November 1993, Dick Spring, the party leader, outlined 'six principles' on which any settlement would have to be based, which emphasised the need for separate Northern consent to any constitutional change in Northern Ireland.[73] More specifically, the party argued that North–South institutions had to be established to express 'the collective needs and economic logic of the island as a whole' and to 'secure the confidence' of the Irish people before risking a referendum on Articles two and three.

The EU had become a central factor in the Labour Party's framework for 'peace and reconciliation', largely in terms of its potential to transcend the stark alternatives of unionism and nationalism. EU integration was seen as encouraging the emergence of 'one agreed nation for all' that could transcend jurisdictional divisions and state-centred nationalism, i.e., an agreed nation that could be achieved despite continued British presence in the North.[74] Reflecting this, in 1993 Dick Spring, the party leader, speaking as Tánaiste, called on the EU to 'bring its ideals to bear on a serious conflict within its borders' and in 1994, he looked forward to a 'new Ireland characterised by partnership and cooperation', as nationalists and unionists were reconciled as 'fellow citizens of the new Europe' (Encounter/British–Irish Association (BIA) 1993, p. 27).

Fine Gael politicians were less enthusiastic about the implications of EU integration for Irish unity, stressing that EU membership would stabilise North–South and Irish–British politics, leading to a normalisation of relations within Northern

Ireland. During his time as Taoiseach, Garret Fitzgerald encouraged the EU not to remain aloof from the conflict and at the NIF in 1983 the party supported a greater EU role in encouraging reconciliation in Ireland.[75] In 1989, John Cushnahan, a Fine Gael MEP, called for unity in Northern Ireland founded on the ideals of Europe 'so that old rivalries and bitterness can finally be forgotten'.[76] Other party MEPs saw the EU as a 'logical continuation' of nationalist ideas as it was guided by the attempt to strengthen democracy where purely national democratic institutions had begun to lose control.[77]

In the 1990s, this interweaving of pressures for Irish unity with positions on EU integration was intensified. For instance, in the 1992 Labour Party–Fianna Fáil *Programme for Government*, there was a heavy emphasis on 'working for peace' in Northern Ireland, founded on the NIF formulation of unity by agreement and bolstered by regionalisation in Ireland as a whole.[78] There was an emphasis on the rewards of enhanced North–South economic cooperation and the two parties committed themselves to initiating programmes of action to ensure that Ireland, North and South, maximised opportunities arising out of the SEM. It was this government, combining Labour traditions with Fianna Fáil nationalism, which was to build on the all-Ireland nationalist unity that had emerged in the 1980s, extending it to the republican movement and to the new Democratic Presidency in the USA, to build the political conditions for the cessation of military conflict in 1994 (see Chapter Four).

CONCLUSIONS

EU integration brought some significant shifts in the ideological positions of the main parties in Ireland, North and South, away from a focus on conflicts over 'national' jurisdiction and towards a debate on how best to meet the needs of the all-Ireland regional economy in the EU. This was cross-cut – in some ways undermined, in others reinforced by an ongoing commitment to 'national' politics, whether centred on Britain, the twenty-six Counties, or on Ireland as a whole. The political tensions that resulted forced some realignments in

115

political positions, North and South, with potentially significant implications.

At the same time, as EU integration accelerated it also challenged concepts of monolithic 'national' state sovereignty, to a significant degree transforming the ways in which sovereignty was being exercised. The implications of the resulting changes in public policy are discussed in the following chapter.

4

Institutions: contested territory, shared governance

This chapter examines changes in public policy within Ireland, assessing whether there has been significant regionalisation on a North–South basis as a result of EU integration. As with the previous chapter, it is divided into two parts: the first examining the pressures for North–South convergence; the second outlining the pressures for continued and, in some respects, sharpened divergence between state policies. In both these explorations, changes in public policy, North and South, are compared. The chapter ends with an assessment of the overall tendencies.

EU integration has exposed the failings in the state administrations of both North and South and has altered the political context of the national conflict. This reflects tensions between the 'national' politics of states and the regionalist politics of some EU institutions and regional authorities. In Ireland the tension has become a deadlock, between the logic of the national conflict and the emergence of an all-Ireland economic region. Although EU integration has most directly affected socio-economic interests and has had little direct impact on state structures, it has begun to legitimise demands for regional autonomy and started to open up new fields of regionalist political struggle, not least in Ireland. These regionalising pressures are presented first, and then set against on-going North–South division centred on the two national states, before an assessment of the overall tendencies is attempted in the chapter's conclusions.

4.1 NORTH–SOUTH LINKAGING

EU institutions have encouraged a regionalisation of political power in the UK and the Republic. At the same time, EU bodies have redefined the national conflict as an EU concern, and have encouraged the British state to work jointly with the Irish Republic in resolving it, or at least in managing it. This has forced North–South issues further up the political agenda in both jurisdictions, leading to some, albeit limited, adaptation of state policies. These North–South responses are now assessed before embarking on an analysis of countervailing pressures for divergence.

Regionalism and state structures: the UK and the Republic

The UK became more centralised after EU membership but remained regionally and nationally diverse, in some respects increasingly so. To a large degree, this reflected regional economic divergence within the UK. During the late 1970s and 1980s, there was a quadrupling of unemployment disparities between UK regions. The gap between the highest and the lowest regional unemployment rates rose from 2.1 per cent in the years 1959–76 to eight per cent in the late 1980s (MacKay, 1992). Partly reflecting this, groupings such as the campaigns for a Scottish, a Welsh and, in England, a Northern Assembly, argued that regional autonomy was urgently required to prevent sharpening peripherality in the SEM (European Dialogue, 1993; Scott and Miller, 1992). Facing greater deindustrialisation and finding greater opportunities for economic development at the EU level, UK regional interests were being transformed, particularly in areas such as Scotland, Wales, the English North and Northern Ireland which had already experienced at first hand the impact of peripherality in the UK political economy.

Local, county and regional authorities demanded greater autonomy and linked themselves to counterparts elsewhere in the EU. Across the UK, from the Scottish Strathclyde Region to the 'Western Development Partnership' in the south-west, local government, in alliance with the EU Commission, sought greater autonomy to determine economic and social priorities

(Rose, 1992). Wales, for instance, actively sought to link-up with the 'four motors', a pan-EU alliance of regions, giving legal guarantees for joint ventures, innovation and technology transfer.[1] At the same time, Kent in the south-east of England joined with Nord-Pas de Calais in Northern France and the three eastern provinces of Belgium to form the 'Transmanche' Euro region.[2] The associations of Scottish, Welsh and English authorities and the Local Government International Bureau (LGIB) successfully campaigned with the European Commission to ensure that UK representatives to the EU Committee of the Regions could not be appointed by central government, securing the only amendment to the Maastricht Bill in March 1993.[3] Building on this, the Association of Metropolitan Authorities proposed that a Cabinet seat should be allocated to a Minister for the Regions and a Select Committee formed to oversee the workings of local government, arguing for the 'decentralisation to standard regions of as many government activities as possible'.[4]

This redefinition of 'regional' and 'national' interests in the UK was actively encouraged by EU institutions. The EU Commission stressed regional interests in the distribution of EU structural funds and became a useful, and reliable, ally of the UK regions. By March 1993, twenty-six regional and local authorities from the UK had established representations in Brussels.[5] As closer EU integration highlighted the anachronisms of the UK political system, it 'transform(ed) the regional problem from a merely economic one to a political and institutional one' (Bogdanor, 1992, p. 8): in 1991 for instance, the government's own Audit Commission argued that 'without effective regional groupings the UK (would) lose out' in the SEM (Audit Commission, 1991, p. 40).

In response to pressures from the EU for greater coherence in UK regional policy, regional planning groups were recreated by the Thatcher government in 1988, nine years after they had been abolished. In 1991, provision was made in the Planning and Compensation Act for local authorities to combine together in order to draw up regional plans; in 1992, the Department of the Environment began encouraging the formation of regional planning fora in each of the 'standard regions'[6] and in 1993, regional aid programmes were decentralised to inter-departmental committees based in new 'standard region' offices.[7] At the same time, increased support for the Labour Party-backed 'Constitutional Convention' in Scotland and for the Scottish Nationalist Party, led to the government's 'taking stock' exercise in Scotland, under which greater powers were devolved to the centrally controlled Scottish Office and a consultative Grand Committee for Scotland was created, forging what the government called a 'partnership for good'.[8]

In the Republic, EU integration also stimulated political debate on the lack of regional government. As elsewhere, EU encouragement of regionalisation highlighted the issue of regional autonomy, as much a political issue, as a purely socio-economic issue. In 1987, the EP adopted a report that high-lighted the centralised structure of the Irish state and the need for regional bodies that could 'promote their region nationally and internationally and stimulate the fullest use of the region's indigenous resources' (European Parliament 1987, p. 8). In 1988, the government was forced, under pressure from the Commission as well as the Parliament, to establish regional advisory bodies to oversee the distribution of EU funds, one year after Regional Development Organisations had been cut to save on travel expenses.[9] These bodies were composed of the various 'social partners' involved in drawing up national economic programmes – 'basically a forum for principal vested interests' rather than elected representatives.[10] The exercise of 'partnership' under the 1989–93 Structural Funds Programme was 'widely seen as window dressing' (Matthews, 1994, p. 49), and partly in response, a joint Commission and government process was established to oversee the participation of sub-regional units in the management of the plan.[11]

In 1993, there was considerable pressure on the Fianna Fáil–Labour Party government to strengthen local government in order to ensure that there was meaningful consultation for the second National Development Programme (NDP) and these issues formed a central plank in its 'Programme of Government'.[12] In 1993, consultation on the 1994–99 NDP with regional bodies and unrepresented 'social partners' was conducted with some care to ensure that the Department of Finance did not impose its own existing priorities on the process. Western regions, in particular, gained a higher political profile in the consultation process, to the extent that TDs, Senators and the local church organised a campaign for 'the West', based in Galway, and visited the Commission in Brussels to put their case forward for improved funding for the region.[13]

Despite state centralisation in the UK and the Republic, the issue of strengthening sub-state structures had become a key political priority in both jurisdictions. Policy implementation by EU institutions and the broader process of integration into the SEM were major factors in this process of democratising and strengthening regional, county and city authorities.

EU interventions and Anglo–Irish cooperation

In Ireland this regional restructuring has involved cross-border and all-Ireland linkaging. Along with closer Anglo–Irish coordination, North–South linkages were viewed as necessary elements in any resolution of the national conflict, which itself was increasingly defined as not simply a British and Irish issue, but as an EU issue. The EP in particular, defined the conflict as not simply a 'domestic' issue for the British government to resolve, but as a matter of legitimate concern for all Europeans. The conflict was seen as undermining Community ideals and as early as 1983, Commission officials described it as a 'blot on the community'.[14] From its first session, the EP questioned British policy in the North and from 1981 passed several resolutions critical of the British government. In the early 1980s, as the conflict escalated, these interventions intensified, and in 1984 the EP's Haagerrup Report identified Northern Ireland as one of the most serious problems facing the EU (European Parliament, 1984). In response, officials from the Commission discussed the possibility of greater involvement and, in the later 1980s, argued that a direct role for EU institutions 'would offer a much better hope of a long-term solution than anything which anyone has yet suggested' (Temple-Lange, 1988, p. 252).

These interventions were driven by a concern to remove the significance of intra-EU borders, as part of the move to reconciliation in a Europe of federalised regions, rather than any specific concern to support Irish nationalism. In the early 1980s, the Parliament passed several resolutions condemning breaches of the European Convention on Human Rights in Northern Ireland for instance, concerning the use of plastic bullets, the practice of strip searching, the use of supergrasses and the deterioration in prison conditions. But at the same time, in 1982 it urged the Republic to sign the European Convention on Terrorism to enable South–North extradition, arguing that 'there can be no justification for the use of force against a democratic society'; it viewed national criteria on 'political' and 'non-political' crime as a hangover of 'old nationalistic concepts', and requested pan-EU measures to increase 'mutual assistance in criminal matters, the compellability of witnesses, the taking of witness statements and the transfer of prisoners'.[15] In later years, it condemned IRA atrocities such as the Enniskillen bombing and welcomed the AIA as a step towards reconciliation between the two member states.

Such interventions were consistent with other assertions of EP jurisdiction in relation to the conflict. The 1985 decision of the Political Committee to overrule the objections of the UK Committee of Permanent Representatives of the member states of the EU (COREPER) and appoint Nils Haagerrup as an official rapporteur on the political situation in Northern Ireland, granting him uniquely broad terms of reference, was influenced by this determination to map out the Parliament's right to intervene on such issues. This defined the conflict as a matter of legitimate concern at the EU level, underlined by MEPs who argued that opposition to 'interference in internal affairs is a relic of the old and outdated traditional concept of national sovereignty' (this contrasted with the inter-governmentalist European Political Cooperation, where the topic had been a 'taboo' subject).[16]

This had significant effects on British–Irish relations, as 'macro-regional' EU institutions established a degree of international legitimacy for the Republic's position in the conflict (Keatinge, 1991; Coughlan, 1992). EU membership enhanced the Republic's international status and Partition became less of a symbol of the South's subordination, instead becoming more a symbol of zero-sum British nationalism in the face of positive-sum Euro-regionalism (Guelke, 1988, p. 164). Indeed, direct political pressure from EU institutions encouraged the emergence of an 'EC engendered trust' between the Irish and British governments and provided the practical basis for Anglo–Irish inter-governmental dialogue on the North, seen by both governments as an alternative to more extensive EU intervention in the conflict.[17]

As early as 1977, meetings between representatives of the two states on the sidelines of the European Political Cooperation (EPC) and the European Council offered a private, multilateral setting for relations between the UK and the Republic. This gave the two states greater room for manoeuvre as neither were required to make 'public affirmations of their government's respective position on the constitutional issue', in contrast with the bilateral framework which bound the states into a direct relationship in the glare of media publicity.[18]

In 1985, this was formalised in the AIA, which institutionalised Anglo–Irish relations and defined the conflict as largely the concern of the two state powers. The agreement won widespread acclaim from EU institutions, which subsequently contributed to the 'International Fund for Ireland' which had been set up by the USA to improve community relations in the north of Ireland, including the border regions.[19] As a by-product, ironically, the AIA delegitimised any further EU interventions.[20] The two states had come to an agreement that they would jointly manage the conflict as an issue of common concern. The UK would exercise sovereignty, while the Republic was entitled to protect 'its' minority in the North, in consultation with the UK government, thereby curtailing the directly political role of EU institutions. Partly as a result of this, after devoting 'an unusual amount of time and energy' to the Northern Ireland issue in the early 1980s, from 1985 EU institutions maintained a relatively low profile on Northern issues.[21]

More positively, exposure at the EU level had a direct impact on the management of the conflict. In effect, the British government had been forced to take 'international opinion' into account, leading it into closer cooperation with the government of the Republic (Rolston, 1991). Under the AIA, the two states recognised that the conflict was an international issue involving the two states and the two parts of Ireland, as much as an internal problem involving nationalists and unionists. As the British Foreign Secretary stated in 1985, 'no sense (could) be made of the politics of Northern Ireland within the confines of Northern Ireland'.[22]

This partial relaxation of national state sovereignty in a multilateral, regionalist context broadened the range of constitutional options being considered by the two governments and by participants in the conflict – options that 'offered some hope for reconciliation' – as the British Foreign Secretary put it, in 1994.[23] In particular, joint government action to increase North–South integration, perhaps through all-Ireland institutions with executive powers, became more of a possibility, even in the absence of significant transfers of constitutional sovereignty. This increased Anglo–Irish political cooperation to some degree succeeded in insulating Britain from direct political interventions from the EU. But it did not prevent interventions on socio-economic policy, which in several respects encouraged the redefinition of Ireland, North and South, as a single EU region.

EU pressures for North–South integration

EU institutions highlighted Northern Ireland's socio-economic problems, legitimising and financing initiatives to hasten North–South socio-economic integration. Initially this took the form of simply providing extra funds for Northern Ireland. In 1981, MEPs emphasised that 'the desire for peace is closely linked to living conditions and employment' and called for special attention to be given to the region. The resulting report on regional development in the North received the support of all three Northern MEPs because, as the DUP MEP put it, it confined itself to 'social and economic' issues rather than touching on the 'political and constitutional affairs of Northern Ireland'.[24]

This contrasted with the two unionist MEPs' condemnation of the Haagerrup Report in 1984, which was seen as politically motivated and as stepping beyond the ambit of EP responsibility, into the realm of state jurisdiction, thereby constituting 'a deliberate interference in the political and constitutional affairs of Northern Ireland'.[25] The report also attracted the opposition of the British Conservatives, to the regret of at least one of their number, Fred Catherwood. Partly due to this, the

European Commission declined to adopt a directly political profile on the conflict and instead continued to offer 'exceptional' EU funding for Belfast, on this occasion amounting to ECU 100 million for an 'integrated operations' programme in Belfast, granted on the express condition that the money was to be formally 'additional' to existing public expenditure in the North.[26]

This pattern of offering economic support rather than exerting political pressure was repeated later in 1984 when the EP welcomed the Anglo–Irish process and again called for more funds to be directed to the region. This resulted in the 'integrated rural development programme' outlined in the Maher Report of 1986.[27] Again, this report failed to receive the support of unionist MEPs, not for its recommendations but for its political content – in particular, its praise of the AIA. The UUP MEP John Taylor complained, 'we need democracy in Northern Ireland, not outsiders interfering in our affairs', a familiar theme, resting on a notional division between the realm of 'legitimate' EU responsibility in economic and social affairs and the 'non-legitimate' interference in political and constitutional matters.[28]

But rather than offering a depoliticised, non-contentious avenue for EU involvement, these funding régimes directly raised issues at the heart of the national conflict. Despite their insignificance relative to the British subvention, the distribution of structural funds highlighted the failures of UK policies in the North and, in the context of intensifying concerns about Northern Ireland's prospects within the Single Market, legitimised the demand for North–South integration.

The issue of 'additionality' in particular directly politicised the British–Northern Ireland relationship as central control of EU funds by Whitehall contradicted their intended role in serving regional interests. There was heavy pressure on the NIO to 'integrate' expenditure of EU funds into the government's expenditure bloc – unless incoming funds were processed by the Treasury and used to meet elements of the UK expenditure plans, they would fail to appear as a credit item in the Treasury accounts.[29] This did not find favour with the Commission, and when the 1989–93 National Development Plan failed to attract any 'new money', the NIO was accused of trampling over the interests of Northern Ireland in favour of what were defined as UK-wide 'national' interests.[30]

The bulk of the regional funds were used to finance infrastructure projects often already in the Northern Ireland expenditure plans (accounting for twenty-four per cent), or were channelled through government quangos such as the IDB and the LEDU. Most European Social Fund (ESF) finances were directed into existing government training projects managed by the Training and Employment Agency (eighty-four per cent of overall funds, comparing with seventy per cent for UK). Similarly, between 1973 and 1987, over eighty per cent of European Investment Bank loans went to public enterprises, such as the state-owned Shorts, Northern Ireland Electricity and British Telecom. Only rarely did locally controlled organisations obtain direct access to EU funds. Northern local authorities were responsible for one per cent of all EU funded projects while in Britain they were responsible for eighteen per cent, and the voluntary sector in the North gained access to fourteen per cent of ESF funds, while in Britain this sector was responsible for thirty per cent (NIEC, 1992).

As the debate about additionality abated – in February 1992 the Regional Affairs Commissioner, Bruce Millan, stated he was 'satisfied' with the additional impact of community aid in Northern Ireland' – the related issue of subsidiarity intensified. This focused attention on the question of whether UK public expenditure priorities met the needs of Northern Ireland as a region in the SEM rather than simply as a region of the UK, or more controversially, simply met the short-term needs of the British state.[31]

Agriculture provided the clearest evidence of this divergence in policy priorities between the UK government and Northern Ireland. British government policies reflected the relative insignificance of the farming sector and Britain's position as a net importer of foodstuffs. When the relatively powerful farming lobby in Britain pressured the government to respond to its needs, it acted in the farmers' interests, reflecting the commodity composition of British rather than Northern Ireland agriculture. This contrasted with the government in the Republic where, as the NIF pointed out in 1984, 'the position adopted by Irish Ministers for Agriculture in relation to improved support prices under the CAP has been more helpful to farmers . . . in the North than the position adopted by the UK ministers'.[32]

Northern Ireland farmers quickly became dependent on the Republic's efforts to shape the EU budget, a process of 'free-riding' on EU concessions (O'Cleireacain, 1983). This was recognised by the EP as early as 1981, when it argued that 'the Republic of Ireland and Northern Ireland form a single economic unit in terms of agricultural production . . . [and hence] proposals relating to special measures for the Republic of Ireland should be extended to cover Northern Ireland'. Concern at the lack of 'fit' between local interests and official structures, reinforced by a sense of political isolation in the North, stimulated interest in alternative routes to Brussels – as a Northern farming magazine argued in 1984, 'second-hand representation simply does not work'. Resentment at the UK government was fuelled by its refusal to match the Republic's level of support to dairy farmers through the 'milk quota', preferring instead to allocate the quota on a UK-wide basis. The dispute remained unresolved as it raised the issue of distributing agricultural assistance on a basis of need rather than on a 'national' basis – an approach that the UK government had consistently vetoed in the Council of Ministers. The result in the North was a falling quota of milk output, amounting to a 6.5 per cent cut in 1984 and a ten per cent cut in 1988, while in the Republic quotas rose by 4.6 per cent in 1984, although in 1990 they fell 3.9 per cent.[33]

Partly as a result of a growing divergence between Britain and Northern Ireland, accompanied by increasing commonalities between Northern and Southern interests, the conceptual divide between 'non-political' socio-economic intervention and more directly political forms of intervention became increasingly difficult to sustain, especially as EU funding régimes became aimed at meeting the common needs of the island economy. Significantly, such political interventions could not be deemed to be 'too political' by either member state, as EU institutions could claim they were under a direct responsibility to initiate and encourage North–South cross-border integration as part of the process of integration into the 'borderless' SEM.

This redefinition of Ireland as a single regional unit was first pursued by Irish MEPs in 1979 who raised the issue of economic integration in Ireland and called on the Commission to distribute funds on an all-Ireland basis.[34] From 1982, EU Commissioners highlighted the need for Ireland, North and South, to act together at the EU level and to draw up joint development plans that recognised the common needs of the two parts of Ireland.[35] In October 1982, it was proposed that a joint EU development committee should be established, based in Belfast, Derry and Dublin, working to an 'Action Plan' to maximise the benefits of the EU for Ireland as a whole (this was never implemented).[36] In 1991, as the SEM completion date loomed, the Commission openly advocated the need for North–South institutions to address the political issues raised by closer economic integration; and in 1993, it proposed that there should be a specific North–South component to the structural funds programme in the two parts of Ireland.[37]

This pressure was, to some extent, consistent with the two governments' existing commitments. In 1976, the UK and the Republic had submitted requests for funds under the European Regional Development Fund (ERDF) regulations to finance half of the cost of studies into the Derry–Donegal area, and under the European Agriculture Guidance and Guarantee Fund (EAGGF) to fund projects at the Mourne Fisheries and in the Erne catchment area. The two governments commissioned 'Joint Studies' to assist them in the 'special consideration of the totality of the relations within these islands'; a joint steering group was established to manage the projects and ECU 8 million was spent from 1979 to 1984.[38] EP pressure helped to ensure that this was extended in 1980 and again in 1985, when the Council of Ministers agreed specific regulations to permit expenditure 'to improve the economic and social situation in Ireland's border areas', primarily in the tourist industry. The Commission also authorised a contribution to Cooperation North, a body that began working on North–South issues in the early 1980s. In 1986, in the wake of the AIA, it contributed ECU 15 million to the 'International Fund for Ireland'; two years later it created a unique fund for 'reconciliation' projects in Northern Ireland as part of the Northern Ireland section of the UK National Development Plan.[39]

In all of these cases of cross-border assistance, the EU integration process provided the framework within which they could be agreed, in effect, giving a 'fillip to cross-border cooperation' (European Parliament, 1979). Where they required joint coordination, the programmes of expenditure were progressed through the Anglo–Irish intergovernmental committees set up after 1981 and through the Maryfield secretariat of the AIA from 1986.

In 1990, this funding régime was formalised on an EU-wide basis as a 'Commission Initiative' aimed at assisting border regions, the INTERREG programme, which established a regular bidding and allocation mechanism which was said to have 'unrivalled support' at the Council of Ministers. INTERREG required the creation of a 'monitoring committee' composed of officials from both jurisdictions and from the Commission; in the case of Ireland, this was established in September 1991 as a North–South Steering Committee of civil servants and Commission officials. Chaired jointly by the Department of Finance (Dublin) and the Department of Finance and Personnel (DFP) (Belfast), and operating under the aegis of the Anglo–Irish Intergovernmental Conference, this further legitimised joint working on cross-border initiatives.[40]

This shift towards treating North and South as one unit was not reflected in the community support frameworks drawn up by the two governments for the period 1989–93, despite the two regions being awarded 'Objective One' status. Although the Commission began liaising with the two governments from the same office in Brussels, the two governments devised their programmes separately, and there was no attempt at cooperation or coordination. Throughout the entire funding period, the allocation for INTERREG, which amounted to ECU76 million for both North and South during 1991–93, was not integrated with either of the governments' spending plans. Furthermore, in contrast with all other EU regions eligible for INTERREG funds, the money was allocated without detailed information on which proportion would be spent in the North and which in the South.[41] In contrast, the plans for the 1994–99 tranche of structural funds allowed for joint North–South action. These developments are discussed in what follows, focusing first on changes in state policy in the North.

North–South convergence: Northern Ireland and the Republic

In Northern Ireland there was a partial but significant shift away from regional planning on a solely Northern Ireland or UK basis, towards greater consideration of North–South development issues. A key factor in this shift was the recognition that, in order to be effective, government priorities for EU funding régimes had to be developed in 'partnership' with business, community, local authority and other social actors in Northern Ireland. The storm of controversy precipitated by the process of drawing up the 1989–93 funding programme contrasted with the relative consensus that had been built up around the 1994–99 priorities.

This relative openness in the policy-making process, in contrast to the closed process of drawing up wider public expenditure priorities in Northern Ireland, ensured that North–South dimensions were forced onto the agenda. Non-government, business-orientated organisations played a key role in legitimising this approach. The NICE helped to organise two consultative conferences on the issue of structural funding, with the Northern Ireland Department of Finance and Personnel in December 1992 and with the European Commission in October 1993. At the first of these conferences, the need to free the Northern economy from its slow-growth British neighbour was highlighted and it was argued that Northern Ireland had to build on North–South 'complementarity' to exploit substantial and as yet, missed opportunities for improving links within the 'island as a whole' (DFP 1992, p. 42). The advantages of such North–South coordination, as against pursuing similar objectives in separation, were seen as extending beyond the one-off benefits of infrastructure improvement into the dynamic benefits of the 'close and interactive synergy' of an island economy (DFP 1992, p. 92). By placing Northern Ireland's regional development in a transnational EU context, Northern Ireland was redefined as a region in the EU rather than simply as a region of the UK, making North–South, all-island development not just possible, but desirable. As the NICE argued, at the second conference, integration into the EU 'must necessarily pose the question of closer cooperation with the Republic of Ireland'. This mapped out a new agenda for economic policy in the North that, strikingly, forced government representatives to defend their record on improving North–South linkages (NICE, 1993).

In the subsequent funding round, Northern Ireland and the Republic both remained 'Objective One' regions, and more important in terms of the distribution of the funds, there emerged a new interest in North–South development. In the 1993 Structural Funds Plan (SFP) for Northern Ireland, external cohesion, defined as cohesion with the Republic as well as with the wider EU, was identified as one of the three strategic objectives for economic development in the North, along with economic growth and internal cohesion. Given Northern Ireland's relative peripherality, it was suggested that improved linkages with trans-European networks would be a key factor in the development of the Northern Ireland economy. These included improved networking 'on a territorial basis' with the contiguous Southern economy, to reap the benefits of greater economic integration on 'the island of Ireland'. This required 'a strategic framework . . . [to] take account of the benefits of developing and strengthening mutually advantageous linkages within the island of Ireland' (HMSO, 1993, p. 39–41).

This strategic overview of the Northern economy, in which linkages with the Republic were defined as a key element in the overall development package, was a significant new departure for the Northern Ireland government. Economic relations with the Republic had been acknowledged as an important issue since 1989 but they had been restricted to the funding regime under INTERREG, and their implications had not been reflected in the overall framework for the 1989–93 Development Plan. By 1993, in contrast, relations with the Southern economy had become a central element in the programme's strategic overview.

But this innovative strategic framework lost its lustre when translated into operational programmes. Relations with the Republic did not figure in the main programmes and instead were discussed in a separate chapter that had been drawn up jointly between the two governments. This new chapter on 'Cooperation with the Republic' highlighted a number of general non-specific commitments and current activities and could be read as a self-congratulatory rewriting of history, in which both governments were seen to have pursued cooperation, assisted by the Commission.

Despite the high profile accorded to linkages with the Republic, commitments to North–South integration were not written into any of the priorities or programmes, under which the bulk of the structural funds were allocated. Rather than specifying how such strategic North–South issues would be addressed, the plan stated that 'all regional priorities may contribute' to the strategic theme of cross-border coherence (HMSO, 1993, p. 91). In practice there was no mention of the Republic in any of these priorities, beyond what had already been committed, and within the sectoral programmes there was reference only to the familiar themes of the need for enhanced transport and energy links.[42] Otherwise, it was left to the reader's imagination just how far these overwhelmingly Northern Ireland-focused priorities had any relevance for 'cross border coherence'.

The Single Programming Document (SPD) confirmed these suspicions. It made no mention of the Republic, of transport, tourism, technological development or of training, while on energy, it highlighted the agreement to fund separate gas and electricity interconnectors to the UK. The only reference to the Republic was a picture of the Fruit of the Loom factory which showed the Donegal hills in the background and the only reference to the border areas was in relation to INTERREG. Additional information on this initiative was to appear in a subsequent publication – a clear indication that relations with the South would be kept separate from the overall structural funds programme (HMSO, 1994).

This relatively restricted, although changing, situation contrasted with developments in the South. In the Republic, politicians had for some time been formally committed to supporting North–South cooperation, primarily in the border areas. By 1992 this had broadened into an all-island perspective as, in the context of the SEM, the government announced its intention to focus on North–South economic relations, suggesting that 'the costs of the current one island/two economy basis of operation in many areas will become a greater drag on economic progress' (DSO 1992b, p. 32).

Reflecting this, under the Republic's 1989–93 NDP there was some, albeit cursory, reference to cross-border all-Ireland development, with the need to stimulate indigenous industry and to construct stronger North–South linkages. Joint 'mutually beneficial' North–South initiatives were seen as 'essential to optimum economic development in the island as a whole' (DSO 1988, p. 15). But in practice, concrete action was restricted to participation in the INTERREG programme which played a minimal, symbolic role in raising the profile of North–South development issues.

In the early 1990s, the agenda began to shift. In 1992, the report of the Industrial Policy Review Group was critical of the government's continued failure to stimulate indigenous industry (the 'Culliton Report'). This was followed by the government's report on 'Economic Cooperation on the Island of Ireland in an integrated Europe' which suggested that the 1994–99 development plan should more clearly address the need for indigenous development on a North–South basis (DSO 1992a, 1992b). In 1992, Mary O'Rourke, the Minister for Trade in the Republic, announced that cross-border schemes under the joint North–South chapter in the NDP would be a high priority for the Fianna Fáil–Labour Party government. Subsequently a government official confirmed that this approach was shaping government policy, stressing, 'we believe that, by pooling our limited resources in appropriate areas and developing an island-wide approach, we can build on our strengths and maximise the gains for the two economies, North and South'. More specifically, in 1993, Eithne Fitzgerald, Junior Minister of Finance responsible for the NDP, stated that the Republic was committed to extending inter-departmental links and to identifying 'areas where joint approaches or parallel actions can be mutually beneficial and to ensure in so far as possible that our development priorities are complementary'.[43]

As a result, the Republic's 1994–99 NDP attempted to elaborate possible North–South dimensions for most of the seven priority areas for structural funds investment. The industry chapter, for instance, included a sub-section on joint working with Northern Ireland, identifying the need for joint product promotion, import substitution and research collaboration, while the 'human resources' chapter proposed joint working on vocational education and training and on technology transfer (DSO 1993, p. 94). The government saw this, and the joint North–South chapter, as a 'significant cross-border element' but, as with the Northern Ireland plan, serious consideration of how such issues were to be addressed were postponed until the details of the INTERREG programme had been negotiated.[44]

Indeed, despite the government's announced intention to focus on developing indigenous economic muscle, the strategy of attracting overseas capital was still expected to require over half of the funding available for industrial grants. Nonetheless, this was a significant change from the 1989–93 programme, which allocated thirty-five per cent (IR £145.8 million) of industrial grants to indigenous industry, while the 1994–99 allocated forty-eight per cent (IR £291 million). This was expected to yield growth of 11,000 in employment within indigenous industry, comparing with growth of 9,000 in jobs in multinational corporations (DSO 1993, p. 46). The plans were to be considered 'in conjunction with' the Northern Ireland Plan, but it was not made clear exactly what this would mean for the funding programme.[45] Moreover, in maintaining an externally-orientated approach in tandem with attempts at stimulating domestically owned industry (a 'dual track' approach dating back to the early 1980s) there was every possibility that on-going competition for sources of external capital would disrupt improved North–South cooperation.

Nonetheless, this limited attempt at integrating the two separate development plans was a new departure, and signalled a possible sea-change in official orientations in both juris-dictions. Perhaps more important than its limited content, this North–South joint working had significant symbolic effects, particularly in terms of legitimising practical ad hoc initiatives. In the early 1990s, for instance, building on a history of coop-eration dating back to the early 1980s, the Northern Ireland Tourist Board and Bord Fáilte began cooperating in jointly financing a unified bookings system. Similarly, from 1990, cooperation between the four border Health Boards was intensified, leading to North–South information sharing and joint procurement, saving St£4 million in 1992.[46]

On transport, moreover, there was a substantial shift. This was a particular issue for the South as the Dublin government had routinely ignored the need to improve cross-border transport links: the Republic's national expenditure plans and submissions for EU funding had downplayed North–South linkages since the 1970s, while emphasising Dublin–Cork, Dublin–Wexford and Dublin–Galway transport links.[47] In the 1989–93 structural funds programme, a feasibility study for improved rail links was completed but not acted on and EU funds were instead channelled into transport improvements for the Dublin suburban area. By 1989, the NIO had approved expenditure for the rail project, but it was only with the sustained pressure of Irish business associations, particularly the CII/IBEC Irish Business Employers' Confederation and the CBINI, that the Republic's 1993–99 funding programme confirmed that the Dublin–Belfast road and rail links would be a 'top' priority for investment (DSO 1993, p. 108).[48]

To some degree, then, there was a shift in public expenditure priorities, away from a twenty-six county towards a thirty-two county perspective. To a degree, the Northern government and its Southern counterpart had begun to define their policies in a North–South framework. EU integration had encouraged some movement towards policy-making on an all-Ireland basis but this process depended on EU encouragement and on pressures from non-government agencies, especially business groupings. Consequently, North–South cooperation tended to be piecemeal and disjointed and did little to disengage the North from the UK macro-economy. While there may have been some limited regionalist adaptations of state policy on a North–South, all-Ireland basis, state policies remained focused on the separate 'national' jurisdictions. These counter-pressures encouraging North–South divergence are discussed in the next sub-section.

4.2 NORTH–SOUTH SEPARATING

Despite some limited North–South regionalisation, Northern Ireland and the Republic have retained nationally defined institutions and policies. Against tendencies elsewhere in the EU, centralising pressures have intensified in both the UK and the Republic, partly reflecting on-going constitutional conflicts between them. Analysis of these factors provides the context for a more detailed discussion of the pressures on state policy that cross-cut and undermine North–South regional integration.

State centralisation: UK and the Republic

The Republic and the UK are among the most centralised states in the EU and have been criticised periodically by the Commission on this count. As a constitutional monarchy, the UK state is founded on concepts of the sovereign power of the 'Crown in Parliament', while in the Republic, state authority is linked to a popular mandate, of the 'Irish nation' (Constitution, Article one). The concept of sovereignty that dominates the politics of both countries is thrown into sharp relief by decentralising and federalising tendencies which have become a central feature of EU integration (Loughlin, 1991). Consequently, the two states have tended to act as constraints rather than as 'facilitators' in the regionalisation of state policy, with clear implications for North–South linkages.[49]

In the UK, the British Parliament governs with some administrative powers devolved to local authorities and to appointed administrative elites (Crick, 1991). In the 1970s, proposals to democratise the British system of government were shelved and the 1972 Local Government Act failed to implement the recommendation that England should be administered by five Provincial Councils. Throughout the 1980s and early 1990s, there was a progressive transfer of administrative powers from local government to centrally appointed 'quangos' or to Whitehall. By 1993 there were 77,000 quangos responsible for twenty per cent of public expenditure. Metropolitan Authorities had been dissolved ten years earlier, and the Welsh Counties, some English Counties and nine Scottish Regional Authorities were dissolved in 1993–95.[50]

For the most part, the UK state ignored demands for regional autonomy, reflecting a fear of fragmentation in the heterogenous, multinational, multi-regional UK state – a fear of what the Secretary of State for Scotland called the 'slippery slope' of Home Rule that concerned the power of symbolic images and rhetoric of the state as much as its institutional structures. For instance, when appointed in 1994, the Welsh Secretary required that the Welsh Development Authority use the Union Jack rather than the Welsh dragon in its publicity.[51] Despite EU pressures, the UK moved closer to becoming an 'elective dictatorship', for instance dismantling the Scottish regions and many English counties just as they were gaining recognition at the EU level (Bogdanor, 1992). These democratic deficits were exacerbated in Northern Ireland, where, in 1993–94, local government accounted for UK £194 million or 0.272 per cent of public expenditure.[52] The political consequences of national conflict, the powerlessness of local government, the unaccountability of the NIO and the priority ascribed to security policy had sharpened British state centralism and effectively minimised the impact of EU institutions.

In 1993 the British Government signed up to the concept of 'Subsidiarity,' under the Maastricht Treaty that set up the European Union. This stipulated that public authority should only be exercised at higher levels if this made it more effective. For the British Conservative government this did not apply to the UK, especially in Northern Ireland.[53] Growing awareness of the need for constitutional change, running in tandem with pressures from EU-wide institutions and consistent with the needs of UK regions in the SEM, stimulated a wider debate about the UK constitution. This centred on the need to rekindle democracy, and saw the Labour and Liberal Democrat parties committing themselves to creating regional assemblies in the English regions as well as in Scotland and Wales.[54]

State centralism in the Irish Republic has very different origins. The twenty-six counties have a population of 3.5 million (smaller than many EU regions such as Lombardy and Catalonia), while the UK population is 56.4 million; the Republic was built out of anti-colonial struggle, while the British state was built out of conquest; Ireland has a written Constitution, while Britain's 'unwritten Constitution' is 'vested' in Parliament; people living in the Republic have never demanded the right to secede from the Irish state, while Britain is internally divided between regional and national groupings; finally, state centralism in the Republic is founded on an ideological consensus around 'national' aspirations, while the UK political consensus centres on the sovereignty of the 'Crown in Parliament'.

Reflecting this, many parliamentary politicians in the Republic failed to see centralism as a political issue. In 1990 for instance, the Taosieach, Charles Haughey, anticipated that the existing state structures would 'broadly be kept in place, though perhaps beginning to operate in different ways and through different procedures'.[55] Like the UK, the Republic 'opted out' of the EU-wide tendency to devolve power to sub-state regions. Creeping centralisation can be dated back to the 1960s when regional and local economic policies were increasingly vested in central authorities. This process culminated in the 1969 Buchanan Report which recommended the removal of revenue-raising powers for local government (implemented in 1977), thereby undermining the institutional infrastructure required to service indigenous economic development and to encourage backward and forward linkages between branch plants and the local economy. Later, in 1988, the National Roads Authority took over decision-making on major roads and the Agriculture and Food Development Authority took over responsibility for agriculture. In 1992 an appointed Environment Protection Agency was created.[56]

The Republic has no elected regional authorities and local government is largely conducted through County Councils, whose chief executives are appointed by central government. There are a number of District Councils which, together with the County Councils, exercise minimal local powers. Local authority expenditure stood at five per cent of GDP or 11.3 per cent of total public expenditure in 1990, with key elements of local government – social services, policing and education – run by the central state. Ironically, the first tranche of 'programmed' structural funds was directly managed by the central department of Finance and greatly increased its central powers, reinforcing pre-existing state-centred corporatism. Perhaps not surprisingly, the department then resisted attempts inspired by the EP and led by the Commission at devolving these powers to sub-state regional levels.[57]

Domestic pressures for greater devolution had little success. In 1990, the 'Barrington Report', drawn up by an Irish Commission of Enquiry into Local Government, compared Ireland with EU states, arguing that Ireland had 'lagged behind with overly centralised institutions of government'

(DSO 1990). The report highlighted the abolition of rates in 1977 as the central factor in the declining significance of regional and local government in the Republic. But its recommendations were not acted on as the Fianna Fáil–Progressive Democrat coalition government could not agree on their implementation. In 1991, a local government Bill was introduced, ignoring the Barrington recommendations and giving local authorities the power to nominate to the new regional planning bodies and to twin with other regions in the EU. Two years later the Fianna Fáil–Labour government committed itself to examining regional government, although the issue was again deferred and district elections were not held, as had been promised, at the same time as the European elections, in June 1994.[58]

In general terms, state centralisation associated with conflicting claims to political sovereignty is a key factor in perpetuating divisions in Ireland. Although the North's economic problems are often very similar to the South's and require joint responses, policy coordination is generally ad hoc or non-existent. There was no coherent Northern 'state view' on North–South cooperation across different government departments and there were few joint initiatives by the two administrations (Anderson, 1994). This was exacerbated by competing state claims to territory.

Contesting territory: North and South

The lack of significant adaptation of state policy in both parts of Ireland was at least in part a product of territorial contestation. The British government was committed to maintaining sovereignty in Northern Ireland under the 1800 Act of Union, which decreed that Ireland and Britain would 'for ever be united into one Kingdom' (Article one). The 1920 Government of Ireland Act underlined this commitment, stating that the supremacy of the UK Parliament remained 'unaffected and undiminished over all persons and things in Ireland and every part thereof' (Section seventy-five). The post-Partition Anglo–Irish Treaty recognised the Southern transition to 'dominion' status and decreed that Northern Ireland would continue to be governed under the terms of the 1920 Act (Article twelve). This non-conditional constitutional guarantee set the framework for subsequent clarifications of Northern Ireland's constitutional status. References to the need for 'consent' to constitutional change in Northern Ireland, first defined as the consent of Stormont in 1949 and later, from 1973, of the Northern populace, were seen as a means of strengthening the provisions of the 1920 Act and of confirming North–South divisions in Ireland (Mansergh, 1981).

British claims to territory in Ireland were contested by the Southern state from 1937 when it became a Republic. Its Constitution stated that 'the national territory consists of the whole of the island of Ireland . . .' and claimed 'jurisidiction over the whole of that territory' (Articles two and three). This claim was to be pursued by peaceful means as the Republic was also committed to the 'ideal of peace and friendly cooperation' and to the 'pacific settlement of international disputes' (Article twenty-nine), hence implicitly, it also, accepted the need for Northern consent to reunification. This was clarified in the Sunningdale Agreement of December 1973 when the SDLP and the Republic declared that the 'only unity' they wanted to see was a 'unity established by consent' (DSO, 1973). Later, the AIA of 1985 explicitly expressed this de facto recognition of Partition, in stating that 'any change in the status of Northern Ireland would only come about with the consent of a majority of the people of Northern Ireland' (Article one). At the same time, however, as spelt out by the Irish Supreme Court in 1975 and 1990, politicians in the Republic were required to work for unity as a 'constitutional imperative' (Donoghue, 1993, p. 17).

Pressures from EU institutions, and growing intergovernmentalism at the EU level, encouraged reconciliation between the two states, often, ironically, at the cost of North–South relations. As outlined in Chapter Three, inter-state cooperation encouraged Southern politicians to postpone the pursuit of North–South unity and reinforced the necessity for the unionist community to hold onto its numerical majority in the North. In this context, the Republic was becoming increasingly willing to consider revisions to Articles two and three, as part of a wider package of measures to create structures promoting 'reconciliation between the two traditions and North–South cooperation'. This was greeted with some trepidation amongst nationalist communities in the North, where the constitutional commitment has 'enormous emotional significance' (Donoghue, 1993, p. 18).

Primarily because of these competing claims to sovereignty, but also exacerbated by state centralisation, NIO attempts at establishing limited contacts with the Southern administration were instantly politicised. Under the auspices of the Coordinating Committee of the Anglo–Irish Intergovernmental Council (AIIC), Northern unionists argued that contacts established before the AIA presented a profound threat to British sovereignty in Northern Ireland. During a Northern Ireland Assembly hearing in 1983, the Permanent Secretary at the Department of Finance and Personnel insisted these talks were a routine matter and were 'along the lines of similar arrangements between member states of the European Community' and were no cause for alarm. Unionist members of the assembly remained opposed, arguing that 'economic cooperation is being used as the first stage on the way to . . . political cooperation'.[59]

Despite these concerns, by 1986 inter-ministerial councils had been established under the AIA. These agreed a programme of joint meetings between the Commission and civil servants to develop cross-border projects – joint meetings which were later used to manage INTERREG expenditure.[60] This inter-ministerial control of EU funding programmes was aimed at minimising the involvement of Northern nationalists and unionists. This was in clear breach of Commission funding regulations, established in 1988, which stated that funding programmes should be devised and managed in close 'partnership' with 'authorities', designated by the member states 'at the national, regional, local, or other level', as well as with the Commission.[61] Attempts at 'depoliticising' North–South cooperation kept it in the hands of the two governments, and directly led to the exclusion of local community groups and local politicians from the process of determining priority projects or of managing EU expenditure (O'Dowd, 1993). Such control stifled North–South linkages, ensuring they were restricted to playing a symbolic, legitimising role rather than meeting the urgent needs of the single island economy.

North–South divergence: Northern Ireland

The increasing 'Irish dimension' of British administration in Northern Ireland during the early 1990s was combined with various British government announcements that appeared to signal a 'a major change of tone' in the British position, reflecting a 'deep-seated desire to have less and less to do with Northern Ireland'.[62] In November 1990, the Secretary of State, Peter Brooke, declared that Britain had 'no selfish strategic or economic interest' in Northern Ireland, and two years later, in December 1992, there was acknowledgement of Irish nationalism's legitimate aspirations and grievances, coupled with a recognition that the British record had not been exemplary. The British government more clearly defined itself as an impartial 'facilitator of the expression of democratic will in Northern Ireland'. This defined the British state as a blameless and modest peacekeeper, and suggested, as the Secretary of State put it in July 1993, that the 'challenge and the task for the nationalists in both parts of Ireland is to work towards winning the consent of the unionists', not to persuade Britain to leave.[63] The republican movement was therefore mistaken in targeting the British state, or seeking to influence British public opinion.

This formula was clarified to the IRA during secret negotiations in 1993 and was probably a major factor in securing the ceasefire. In its statements, the government cast itself in an open-ended role of facilitator for reconciliation in Ireland stating that it had 'no blueprint'. The stress on comprehensive agreement – 'the totality of relationships in these islands' – set the context for the assertion that Britain would 'continue to uphold the union' as long as Northern consent to constitutional change was lacking. This new context for Northern consent suggested that a range of measures, perhaps including North–South institutions, could be progressed as part of a general process of reconciliation in Ireland as a whole.[64]

During interparty talks on the North in September 1992, the British government distinguished three approaches or 'models' for North–South bodies: cross-border 'middle ground' institutions; 'transcending' all-Ireland institutions, and institutions 'integrating' the two jurisdictions. These would be answerable to both the Irish and British governments, or to a North–South executive nominated by the Dáil and a Northern Assembly. The proposals were blanketed in the EU context, as the document stated they were aimed at encouraging an 'agreed Ireland' and at 'optimising the benefits of the EC framework for the two parts of Ireland'. Initially UUP politicians were 'favourably disposed' to the proposals, until the end of 1992, when Jim Molyneaux joined Ian Paisley in demanding that there should be no talk of North–South institutions until the Republic had revoked its territorial claim on the North.[65]

Once unionist politicians had linked progress on North–South structures to wider constitutional issues, the British government quickly asserted that such proposals would have to first be agreed by unionist politicians. The Northern Secretary of State remained (patronisingly) convinced that 'once people start to see what can be achieved by way of better cooperation without in any way diminishing the position of Northern Ireland in the UK, then I think fears dissipate and they take heart and they say that wasn't bad!'.[66] But despite government pledges after the breakdown in political talks, that they would improve North–South policy co-ordination through the Anglo–Irish process, they appeared unwilling to take substantive steps until a firm decision-making framework had emerged.

Similar confusion over whether North–South socio-economic institutions presented a threat to British sovereignty, or were purely 'functional' and could be progressed independently of a wider agreement, surfaced during the Reynolds–Major talks in the autumn of 1993. British government proposals embodied in the 'Focus and Direction' document presented to the Irish government in September of 1993 contained a commitment to establishing North South institutional structures. These were designed to manage the regional economy, and as the Secretary of State argued, would 'not impinge on the sovereignty of Northern Ireland'.[67] The Anglo–Irish 'Downing Street Declaration', issued in December 1993, provided an explicit commitment to promote North–South cooperation at all levels and made it clear that such cooperation could be progressed regardless of whether an agreement to end the conflict was reached, arguing that 'the development of Europe will of itself require new approaches to serve interests common to both parts of Ireland'.[68]

But these ostensibly non-political North–South institutions and the broader development of the North–South relationship were once again made conditional upon unionist consent in the British government's subsequent attempts at clarifying the declaration.[69] Jim Molyneaux claimed that he had had an effective veto on the declaration, filleting out its substantive mechanisms, making it more a declaration of principles than a framework for reconciliation.[70] In February 1994, the Secretary of State argued that North–South institutions could 'help transform the relationship between nationalists and unionists' but stated that only with the agreement of northern unionists could they 'take on an increasingly dynamic role on the island'.[71] In response, somewhat predictably, Unionists voiced 'unalterable' opposition and intensified their hostility, stating that they would oppose the creation of all-Ireland institutions 'on principle', regardless of any amendment to the Republic's constitution.

Further illustration of British ambiguity on the question of North–South structures was to be found on the question of the 'Union' itself. In part, this reflected the need to win UUP votes in the House of Commons, stemming from John Major's 'Shotgun Marriage' with Jim Molyneaux.[72] But government pronouncements on the status of Northern Ireland appeared to be more genuine than purely tactical, particularly as UUP support was guaranteed given the Labour Party's pro-unity position at the time.[73] Significantly, the Prime Minister argued that the Downing Street Declaration provided 'an unambiguous acknowledgement by all concerned of Northern Ireland's status within the UK'. He described himself as 'four square behind the Union' and explicitly ruled out devolution as a step on a slippery path to the break up of the UK, arguing that 'the Union is vital for all parts of the UK'.[74]

In more concrete terms, British government security policy continued to take precedence over any concern to assist the process of North–South integration. As an official of the NIO outlined in 1993, social and economic policies in Northern Ireland were designed to 'complement and reinforce' the security strategy (Bell, 1993, p. 27). This was an important theme of North–South politics and was sharpest in the border areas which were described as 'something of a test case in assessing the links between national sovereignty and territorial sovereignty' (O'Dowd, 1993). As EU integration accelerated, the border was further fortified, serving as a 'national' barrier rather than as a regional contact-point between British and Irish jurisdictions (O'Dowd and Corrigan, 1992). Indeed, yearly expenditure on fortifying the border was more than doubled in the late 1980s; annual spending rose to £30–35 million sterling, totalling £160 million sterling by 1995, spent on 229 new installations. Until the paramilitary ceasefires of 1994, at least eighty of the 300 border crossings were closed, only twenty were 'approved' and the rest were deemed to be 'unapproved', subject to intermittent and often permanent closure.[75]

The British government had adopted a policy of accepting the need for some form of regional integration on an all-Ireland basis, partly to normalise and legitimise the North, while at the same time maintaining what were defined as the core elements of British sovereignty. As a result, a dualism between regionalist policies and 'national' territoriality became a constant theme of North–South politics as 'at every step of consideration of economic integration, the security and political situation in Northern Ireland is seen as a major obstacle' (O'Donnell, 1993a, p. 39). This reflected the continuing logic of British state sovereignty in Northern Ireland, the absolute priority accorded to 'security' related issues, and the perceived necessity to hold the 'Union' together in the face of potential fragmentation.[76] But at the same time, the necessity to maintain coherence in this internally contradictory set of policies forced the British government towards a tentative 'creeping confederalism', challenging 'old ideas of Britishness', with direct implications for the conflict and also for the rest of the UK.[77]

North–South divergence: the Republic

Despite being an enthusiastic advocate of North–South integration, the Republic was prepared to make few practical concessions to improving North–South linkages, especially where its interests diverged from UK state policies. Irish politicians tended to aspire to membership of the 'core' group of Germany, Italy, France and Benelux: 'to be safe in the middle of the pack', as Charles Haughey put it.[78] As a result, the Irish government failed to associate and work with other peripheral, small economies within the EU, including Northern Ireland. In spite of some ad hoc cooperation with the 'cohesion group', it did not want to be associated with 'that peripheral riff-raff'.[79] This was partly motivated by a desire to further loosen dependence on the British economy, as well as the desire not to be defined as a 'peripheral' economy in the Single Market.[80]

Of the wide range of issues that illustrate these tendencies, cross-border trade and exchange rate policy were perhaps the most significant. As noted in Chapter Two, from 1979 the Punt shadowed the Deutschmark rather than Sterling. This created price differentials between Northern Ireland and the Republic, and stimulated a rise in cross-border shopping, from South to North, in April 1987. In response, the government imposed restrictions under which travellers were not entitled to a duty-free allowance for northward visits lasting less than forty-eight hours. This had the immediate effect of cutting retail sales in Northern Ireland by some six per cent and increasing sales in the Republic by two per cent, thus safeguarding jobs in the border areas and raising exchequer revenues by some IR£100 million per year (Foley and Mulreany, 1990; Trimble, 1989a, p. 40). The restrictions were declared to be in contravention of the 1987 SEA by the European Court in 1990, but were maintained in amended form by the Republic's Fianna Fáil Minister of Finance, Albert Reynolds, partly to win votes in the border constituencies.[81]

The ambivalent attitude to addressing issues of North–South regional development was also illustrated in the public debate that followed the collapse of Sterling and its departure from the ERM in October 1992.[82] The Irish government's determination to maintain the value of the Punt within the ERM reflected the aspiration to membership of a German-led 'core' monetary union, and was intermingled with hopes of gaining enhanced independence for the twenty-six Counties from the declining UK economy. The Republic therefore was heavily committed to the ERM and to EMU, regardless of the consequences for North–South relations in Ireland, as reflected in the Taoiseach's confident assurance in 1991 that 'Ireland will be in a position to move to stage three of the EMU with the first groups of countries'.[83]

A five month battle to maintain the value of the Punt followed, which saw the Irish government 'nail its colours to the mast' of the EMU. From the moment that Sterling left the ERM in October 1992, falling in value by some twenty per cent over three months, market speculation placed the Punt under enormous downward pressure. In the ensuing struggle to maintain the currency's value, the government introduced a range of measures: IR£50 million was spent compensating companies exporting to the UK (mostly Irish owned); IR£24 billion was spent by the Treasury buying Punts on the exchange market, and interest rates were increased to fifteen per cent to attract funds into the Punt. These attempts were frustrated as speculators forced the Irish currency back into closer parity with Sterling, leading to a ten per cent devaluation and allowing a nine per cent reduction in the interest rate in February 1993.[84]

Even after the Punt had been 'kicked out into the doghouse with Sterling' Bertie Ahern, the Finance Minister, insisted that although 'we are on the periphery, we have to keep pushing' and Brendan Halligan, Head of the Institute European Affairs in Dublin, maintained that 'the more the community integrates the more we move towards the centre'.[85] Peter Sutherland, the former EU Commissioner, Chair of the Allied Irish Bank, and soon to be GATT President, returned to the familiar themes of the need to de-couple from Sterling, to 'accelerate diversification' from the British economy and 'aspire to the fast lane' of currency union in an EU currency area of low interest rates.[86]

But others were more sobered by the experience. The Tánaiste Dick Spring described it as a 'chastening experience' and voiced 'deep disillusionment with the failure of EC solidarity'.[87] This reflected a growing awareness of Ireland's peripherality in the EU. As one Irish MEP put it, 'access to the benefits of the SEM for Ireland is like access to the most expensive Dublin hotel for all the Irish people' (Higgins, 1992, p. 63). In effect, the aspiration to membership of the 'fast lane' of integration, leaving Northern Ireland to languish in the 'slow lane' with the rest of the UK, was frustrated by the perception, in EU finance ministries and central banks, that the survival of the Punt was of relatively minor importance in the ERM and that the Irish economy was, in any case, still tied to the UK economy.

Sections of the Irish press acknowledged the EU had strengthened the 'core' relative to the 'periphery'. There was growing recognition that the 'buckets of Euromoney will only keep us in our place' and that 'the ironic result of greater unification in Europe would be to make us even more marginal'.[88] Integration into the SEM confirmed that the Republic, along with many other regions in the EU, was on the 'outer periphery' of the SEM. This highlighted the need to maximise Ireland's indigenous economic potential.[89] There was an increasing 'refusal to accept an outward orientated and exploitative model of dependent development' and reflecting this, an increased awareness of the effects of Southern policies on North–South divisions (Munck, 1993, p. 149). As noted earlier, the 1994–99 NDP signalled an increased emphasis on the need to invest public funds in indigenous industry. This was coupled with a new acceptance of the necessity to involve regionally representative bodies in the process of regenerating Irish industry and a new recognition of the necessity to maintain and extend linkages with the Northern economy.[90] As argued by the Taoiseach in November 1993, 'in the context of the Single Market there is immense scope and great opportunity for us to work together North and South in a more friendly and civilised climate'.[91]

This increased emphasis on North–South issues had clear implications for the emergence of an all-Ireland regional economy and, crucially, for political institutions to express this. In November 1993, during discussions with the British government over its response to the Hume-Adams proposals, the Southern government sought an 'institutional framework for practical and effective North–South cooperation and coordination'. This would involve ceding executive powers, allowing the North–South body to be 'the instrument for developing an integrated approach for the whole island in respect of the challenges and opportunities of the EC'.[92]

Overall, state policies in the Republic were undergoing some shifts towards a range of policies more orientated to the needs of indigenous industry based at the sub-regional level and at the all-Ireland level. But, as in the UK, these shifts were piecemeal. They failed even to meet the demands of business élites, North and South, and were undercut by a continued commitment to separate development. As illustrated by the limited, and belated, shifts in public expenditure programmes and economic strategy, reorientations in state policy were centrally dependent upon continued policy development at the EU level and on lobbying by North–South interests. Clearly, a more effective North–South state response to regional integration desperately required stronger institutional guidance, to transform tentative 'ad hocery' into accountable and concerted joint action.

The Republic had primarily seen EU membership as a means of gaining greater autonomy from Britain – a strategy that was primarily aimed at serving the interests of the twenty-six county Republic rather than meeting the objective of North–South unity. As the Republic's accession to the ERM demonstrated, the pursuit of such autonomy and the economic benefits it implied, generally over-rode any legal or constitutional responsibility to enhance all-Ireland unity (Laffan, 1983). Southern governments were signally reluctant to give priority 'to the future citizens of a united Ireland at the expense of the electorate of the present day Republic' (Lyne, 1990, p. 430). Indeed, the more that politicians in the Republic were conscious of the immediate needs of their electors and the more they sought autonomy from the UK within a EU setting, the greater the division between the North and South.

CONCLUSIONS

As with party politics, so with state authority; North–South linkages are influenced by the logic of the national conflict. This 'sensitivity' to the unionist–nationalist divide is overlaid by equally powerful jurisdictional pressures. Partly as a result, North–South initiatives are channelled through intergovernmental structures such as the AIIC and non-representative quangos such as the International Fund for Ireland (IFI), thus surrendering authority on North–South issues to unelected officials, and in the last resort, to private business. Adjustments to the policies of the two governments remained largely piece-meal, these were contradicted by 'national' macro-economic policies and were stalled by over-centralised administrative structures, North and South. Yet North–South socio-economic integration urgently needed political direction. The more ambitious proposals for policies to create a 'synergy' of economic interests in order to exploit the more dynamic opportunities offered by the SEM required institutional guidance, and the process of defining economic policy for the island as a whole required accountable North–South decision-making structures.

As the costs of maintaining North–South divisions escalated, in terms of opportunities lost as well as in terms of existing commitments, and as the two governments conceded the need for mutual compromise between the states' constitutional claims, it became possible to conceive of new institutional frameworks which could supersede the existing, stunted constitutional division. Indeed it was on this basis that the British government floated proposals for a partial transfer of authority to all-Ireland economic institutions during the talks process in 1992 and that the SDLP in the North, the Irish Labour Party-Fianna Fáil coalition in the South and sections of the British Labour Party argued for joint Irish–British structures as the political expression of common interests on the 'island of Ireland' (O'Leary, 1993).

For the Republic, the key issue was not so much whether it should postpone socio-economic aspirations in favour of political aspirations, but rather whether the process of pursuing its objectives within a twenty-six county framework would become consistent with the process of strengthening all-Ireland unity. The phase of EU integration in the early 1990s began to have this effect, leading politicians in the Republic to recast twenty-six county state policy into a thirty–two county mould. Meanwhile, as British state policies in the North were placed in the context of increasing demands for North–South economic integration, there was a limited, but nonetheless significant, 'redefinition of Britishness', embodied in the Downing Street Declaration and, associated with this, tentative moves towards building stronger North–South linkages.[93]

5

Conclusions

This book has outlined deep tensions and contradictions between EU integration and the national conflict in Ireland. The Republic is the only former colony among EU member states and the political culture of Ireland continues to be dominated by nationalisms claiming both colonialist and anti-colonialist lineages. Across the island political affiliations are shaped by conflicts over state jurisdiction and territorial affiliation, with most political parties organised on national rather than on class lines. At the same time, both Northern Ireland and the Republic are subject to growing regionalisation both at EU and all-Ireland levels. North and South are highly dependent on EU multinational capital and the South is more locked into EU trading patterns than any other member state. Partly because of internationalisation, but also because of the pressures arising out of integration into the Single Market, North and South are increasingly defined as constituting a 'single island economy'. These pressures disrupt political constituencies and challenge established party political positions. Across the EU, national politicians are forced to confront sharp tensions between 'national' questions and the process of EU integration, and in this Ireland is no exception.

The process of integrating Ireland into the EU has generated powerful socio-economic imperatives. These highlight North–South economic divisions, pose dilemmas for political actors and require the construction of North–South systems of institutional regulation. In the context of EU integration, there has been an emerging consensus that public intervention is required at the all-Ireland level, as well as at other levels, if the two parts of Ireland are to survive in the emerging 'Single Market'. In this book these pressures have been discussed across the categories of interests, ideologies and institutions. These are summarised here and the wider possibilities, primarily in terms of party politics and institutional change, are debated. The book ends with some assessment of how these developments help to explain the 1998 Peace Agreement.

By the early 1990s, the process of EU integration was beginning to legitimise the concept of the 'one island economy' as a central component of socio-economic development in Ireland. Integration into the SEM was stimulating a heightened awareness amongst Southern and especially Northern business interests of the need for greater North–South economic integration. There was a growing orientation towards island-wide concerns, along with significant convergence in socio-economic conditions and structures of business ownership. This was leading to the emergence of an all-island context for business interests, and suggests the possibility of an all-island middle class.

As business organisations make demands for state action in the service of their emerging priorities, a series of agendas for North–South public action have opened up. The business focus of these agendas is increasingly supplemented, and in some ways challenged, by a range of social movement organisations, including trade unions and voluntary, women's and environmental groups. While in 1974, church based organisations were still the strongest North–South social institutions, by 1990, campaigning and advocacy organisations had taken the lead in building cross-border links, primarily to increase their political leverage (Whyte, 1983; Murray and O'Neill, 1991). The North–South dimension is emerging as a new 'framework for disagreement' in Ireland – a framework that has the potential to subvert national divisions and restore social and economic concerns at the heart of North–South relations (see Anderson and Goodman, 1998).

Business enthusiasm for integration is motivated by economic and not political concerns. But as some observers have argued, any serious attempt at economic integration would have to address political issues, including the problem of ensuring accountability to two separate electorates in two separate states and the inevitability of conflicts of interest between them. These factors suggest that integrating the two economies would require concerted political management and joint North–South institutions legitimised by democratic involvement (see Anderson, 1994). These could democratise the North–South policy-making framework, permit access for social groupings other than business organisations and ensure that the emerging system of regulation gains wider legitimacy.

While North–South frameworks may assist economic and social development, these would not, in themselves, resolve the conflict. The process of EU integration has legitimised the concept of the 'one island economy', but practical progress on economic integration is hampered by the divergent policies of the two states and by political divisions associated with the national conflict. As noted in Chapter Three, the conflict dominates the debate on the political implications of integration and creates sharp North–South political divergences. Disputes between nationalists and unionists have emerged over the impact of integration on the national conflict, contrasting with a relative consensus on the need for greater North–South economic integration as part of the EU. Politicians from across the political spectrum have recognised the pressures for economic integration and have adapted their political positions in response to the emerging EU related agendas. A remarkable consensus has emerged on the need for increased North–South economic cooperation, with most Northern politicians sharing fears of peripheralisation in the Single Market and agreeing that EU integration requires a reassessment of economic development policies (Goodman, 1996). The process of reconciling the demands of regional integration with the logic of national conflict sees politicians constructing their own versions of EU integration, accommodating themselves to EU pressures and redefining 'their' national community (Goodman, 1995a).

Politicians have interpreted EU integration in terms of 'national' development and have attempted to limit change according to what 'their' national community is willing to accept. These themes are particularly strong amongst Ulster Unionist and Democratic Unionist politicians, who define unionist or loyalist opposition to any form of political link-up with the Republic as an unchanging fact of political life in the North. Nationalists and republicans, by contrast, emphasise the malleability of political categories in the North, stressing the pressures for North–South integration in the context of the SEM consistent with the aspiration to a more unified Ireland.

The active reproduction of 'national' ideology reflects the continued, indeed in some senses strengthened, significance of nationalisms and national states in the EU. In the face of state disempowerment within a regionalised EU, national ideology has been realigned and reconstructed, not dissolved. But even this process of reproduction induces significant shifts. With heightened integration into the EU there is every likelihood that linkages between Britain and the North will weaken. Partly reflecting this, as pressures intensify from North–South business groupings and other social actors, especially women's groups and trade unions, the static national identity of the Northern unionist community will face formidable internal pressures. Increasingly outflanked by North–South interests, unionist and loyalist politicians have been forced to respond to the increasing demands for North–South cooperation, and have begun to recognise that 'their' communities are by no means monolithically opposed to socio-economic and cultural integration with the South.

There are significant parallels in the reappraisal of nationalist and republican positions. In the early 1990s, there was already a growing acceptance of a mostly regional, and only residually national, future for a reunified Ireland within the EU. National aspirations were being redefined as Irish unity was no longer seen as necessarily requiring all-Ireland national sovereignty; associated with this was an emphasis on the process of national reconciliation, as part of a wider process of integration. The expectation of relatively rapid movement to the fixed outcome of national sovereign independence was downgraded. This enabled greater recognition of the legitimacy of unionist national identity, and acceptance that it is likely to remain a feature of Ireland's political landscape, whether unified or not.

In general terms, dilemmas between 'national' politics and the logic of transnational integration have been forcing political realignments in the national conflict. This reconfiguration of 'national' rhetoric amongst nationalists and unionists possibly signals a shift away from the politics of mutually exclusive 'national' blocs into a more regionalist political rhetoric. It could in turn offer the possibility of strengthening positive-sum *inter*-communal linkages on an all-Ireland basis, against more zero-sum nationalist or unionist *intra*-communal linkages.

The process of ideological adaptation has led to some North–South convergence, and is perhaps the single most important factor encouraging the process of consensual constitutional change in Ireland. EU integration defines positive reasons for Northern unionists to reconsider opposition to some all-Ireland 'unbundling' of state powers; it also pressures nationalists to engage more closely with Northern unionism in a relatively open-ended process of North–South reconciliation. Simultaneously, integration encourages Northern and Southern politicians to refocus their attention on the indigenous development of Ireland as a whole. EU integration thus introduces new political imperatives and opens up new avenues for political change. In doing so, it reshapes political conflicts and potentially defines a process of 'national reconciliation' for Ireland as a whole.

The ideological reorientations are to some extent paralleled by institutional changes. With heightened integration into the Single Market, EU officials and business interests have pressurised both states to increase North–South linkages. Partly as a result the Republic began to recast its state policies in a thirty-two county mould and the British government made tentative moves towards encouraging greater North–South cooperation. The responses were at best minimal, but are likely to accelerate as the costs of maintaining North–South divisions escalate.

The institutional shifts depend largely on the EU's impact on British and Irish conceptions of state sovereignty. With state power partially regionalised both in the EU and on a North–South all-Ireland basis, there has been a significant adaptation of the British doctrine of absolute parliamentary sovereignty and also of the Republic's founding principle of national territoriality. From the 1960s, British government policy wavered from permitting a role for the Republic in the affairs of Northern Ireland to a more British nationalist determination to exclude the Republic from such a role. The EU offered a legitimising framework for the former, institutionalising closer Anglo–Irish relations, and from 1985 this gave the Republic a relatively permanent role in Northern Ireland affairs, both indirectly in consultation with the UK and directly through the Maryfield secretariat of the Anglo–Irish Agreement.

Combined with this there were parallel pressures for greater North–South policy-making and administration, legitimised by the process of integration in the Single Market and by associated EU funding regimes.

These redefinitions set the context for the 1993 Downing Street Declaration, in which the British and Irish governments pledged to work for 'national reconciliation' in Ireland as a whole. In contrast with the 1969 Downing Street Declaration, which was issued unilaterally by the British Prime Minister and declared that the affairs of Northern Ireland were entirely a domestic political issue, the 1993 version was issued jointly by the British Prime Minister and the Irish Taoiseach and constructed a joint Anglo–Irish consensus on the framework for negotiations on the future of Northern Ireland. It reflected Britain's agnosticism on Northern Ireland's constitutional status and offered the possibility of a permanent shift in the direction of de facto, confederalised relations in Ireland. The 1993 Declaration was underlined by the Joint Framework Document which in 1995 outlined an agenda for North–South executive institutions. These would exercise powers in the name of island-wide, reciprocal interests, primarily in the sphere of economic policy, and would form a central component of any eventual settlement. The institutions would de-link aspects of state responsibility from the 'national' state framework and instead define them in a North–South regional framework. In this scenario, North–South integration would benefit both North and South, potentially allowing positive-sum forms of politics to replace zero-sum divisions.

The Peace Agreement

After three years of stalled negotiations, the governments' proposals for North–South institutions were embodied in the Northern Ireland Peace Agreement, signed by Northern political parties and overwhelmingly endorsed by popular referenda held in May 1998. Against a background of peace-time reconstruction in Northern Ireland and an explosion of multinational investment in the Republic, the Peace Agreement underlined the normalisation of North–South relations. In many ways the Agreement was simply one item on the agenda of post-Cold

War peace-making promoted by the USA. But it was also made possible by the 'changes taking place in the wider international system', and most important amongst these was the process of integration into the European Union (Cox, 1998, p. 329). As argued in Chapters Two, Three and Four, European integration played a central role in reversing uneven development in Ireland up to 1994 and in the following four years these tendencies have been underlined.

From 1993 GDP growth rates in the Republic began to consistently outstrip growth rates in the EU. As GDP began rising more than six per cent per annum, some observers began labelling the Republic as a 'celtic tiger', drawing a parallel with the newly industrialising 'tiger' economies of East and South East Asia. Others were more cautious and emphasised the continuing dualisms in the Republic between the haves and the have-nots and between multinationalised and indigenously-owned sectors – divisions that were paralleled in the North (O'Hearn, 1998). The much lauded increases in per capita GDP pushed the Republic well above the threshold for EU structural funds and increased the Republic's EU budget contributions, making it a net contributor to the EU by 1998.[1] In 1998, in the midst of its much publicised economic boom, the Republic began attracting refugees and asylum-seekers in relatively large numbers, many not receiving the welcome they expected in the 'land of open arms'; the resulting debates about racism and the introduction of a Refugee Act to regulate inward migration served to highlight the historical legacies of Irish migration.[2] Economic growth also highlighted continuing dependence and poverty. Between 1987 and 1994 the profit share of national income had risen by ten per cent (at the expense of wages) and the proportion of the country's GDP flowing out of the economy in the form of repatriated profits continued to rise (to fifteen per cent by the late 1990s) (O'Hearn, 1998). The proportion of the workforce on the unemployment register remained at about twenty per cent and the Republic still had the highest rate of long-term unemployment amongst the twenty-nine industrialised countries in the OECD. In April 1997, despite three years of 'tigerhood', the government announced an anti-poverty strategy to address widening inequality and impoverishment.

Whether the Republic was becoming a 'tiger' or not, the North would never regain its historic role of superior indus-trialiser and perhaps would lapse into an even more subsidiary role as a relatively irrelevant backwater. As the Republic joined the Euro, with the British government remaining aloof, possibilities of closer economic integration between North and South appeared to be disappearing. This was confirmed in a Coopers and Lybrand Report of April 1998 which predicted that monetary union without the UK would undermine North–South trade in Ireland.[3] In 1996 Northern Ireland farmers were included in an EU ban against British beef, feared to be con-taminated with BSE (so-called mad cow disease). In a telling move, to police the ban, and to prevent it from being extended to include Southern beef, the Republic set up Garda checkpoints along the North–South border which were later reinforced by mobile military patrols. These were in place from April 1996 to October 1997 while the three Northern MEPs, including the Reverend Ian Paisley, headed delegations to the British Prime Minister and to the European Commission to argue that Northern Ireland beef should be exempted from the ban.[4]

Within Northern Ireland there had been an economic recov-ery from 1994, fuelled by economic growth in Britain and in the South and by the limited influx of international investment that followed in the wake of the 'Peace Process'. By 1997 Northern unemployment had fallen to the lowest level in eighteen years, at 6.9 per cent (although this was assisted by a range of administrative measures designed to take people off the unemployment register). But the underlying structural problems remained, expressed most clearly in the continued absolute dependency on the British Treasury – a dependency that only heightened as the ceasefires made the North more vulnerable to public spending cuts. The process of demo-bilising the Northern war economy highlighted the need for a new economic rationale and the main available option was centred on the possibilities offered by the EU and by improved linkages with the South.

To some extent this found a positive response from Southern élites. In late 1998, for instance, Garret Fitzgerald argued that the South had a responsibility to save the North from the 'fate of a mezzogiorno'. From 1995, disposable income had been greater in the South than in the North, and Fitzgerald argued it was time the Southern government took a 'radical new approach to industrial policy' and joined with the North to attract industry to the island.[5] The message was a familiar one, only now it was tinged with a degree of triumphalism; according to the celebrants of the Southern 'miracle', the tables had turned so that it was now the North not the South that was Ireland's 'mezzogiorno'.

There were also historical continuities in party political realignments. The Agreement signed by most of the Northern political parties in 1998 had crystallised the advancing process of mutual recognition between unionists and nationalists. Pro-Agreement politicians had in effect accepted the quid pro quo struck at Sunningdale twenty-five years earlier: North–South institutions would be created to meet nationalist aspirations, and in exchange a power-sharing Northern Assembly would be set up to express unionist priorities. The British constitutional guarantee would remain in place and the Republic would recognise that unity was conditional upon Northern consent. The main difference with 1973 was that the two states would remove their constitutional claims to sovereignty, basing Northern Ireland's constitutional status solely on popular consent.

Both unionist and nationalist advocates argued the Agreement was a necessary compromise that would strengthen rather than undermine their cause. The main pro-Agreement unionist, the UUP leader David Trimble, argued that unionists would benefit from the Agreement: the Republic's territorial claim was removed, the British guarantee was retained and a Northern Assembly was reestablished. Power-sharing with nationalists and cooperation with Southern politicians through North–South institutions were argued to be important but relatively minor concessions.[6] Similarly, the main republican advocate of the Agreement, Sinn Féin's Gerry Adams, backed it as 'a basis for advancement' and argued it signalled the start of the transitional era in Ireland which Sinn Féin had been working for since 1992. It was accepted that transitional arrangements would fall far short of unity and that this was necessary to gain unionist consent and participation in the interim structures, although this could not extend to a veto over the whole peace-making process.[7]

Pro-Agreement parties had redefined what was acceptable and in the process had permitted some mutual accommodation. But the majoritarian context was still in place and this was well illustrated by anti-Agreement unionists, who argued that a majority of Northern Ireland Protestants had to vote for the Agreement if it was to have any legitimacy.[8] Faced with the prospect of being out-voted in the Northern Ireland referendum, anti-Agreement campaigners had redefined Northern Ireland majoritarianism as communal majoritarianism. In part this was a logical extension of the British government's constitutional guarantee and reflected the new power-sharing framework in which veto powers were granted to the leadership of unionists and nationalist parties in the Northern Assembly. In effect, anti-Agreement unionists had responded to the new framework by repartitioning Ireland, and in doing so exposed how majoritarianism had been redefined, not dissolved.

This repositioning by unionists and nationalists, whether pro- or anti-Agreement, reflected the much wider process of redefining 'official' nationalism in the UK and in the Republic. As noted in Chapter Three, heightened integration into the EU had brought a significant adaptation of the British doctrine of absolute parliamentary sovereignty and also of the Republic's founding principle of national territoriality. In the new context, governments in the Irish Republic, notably the Fianna Fáil coalitions headed by Albert Reynolds and then by Bertie Ahern, sought to redefine and thereby renew Irish national aspirations (Goodman, 1998).

Under the 1973 Sunningdale Agreement and the 1985 Anglo–Irish Agreement the Republic had recognised that Irish unity was conditional upon Northern consent. The Irish Supreme Court interpreted this as constituting de facto recognition of Partition that did not impinge on the Republic's de jure right to Northern jurisdiction, as expressed in the 1937 Constitution. From 1994 this approach was reformulated into a 'one nation, two jurisdictions' model which allowed the Republic to reassert the aspiration to unity, while recognising the reality of Partition. Ahern clarified the position in 1996 as an issue of historical interpretation: 'while we consider that Partition was a grave injustice and contrary to the principle of self-determination, if correctly observed at the time, we cannot ignore the lapse of time and treat Northern Ireland seventy-five years on as if it had never existed'.[9] By taking this stance and later adopting it on behalf of the Irish government, Ahern was separating the claim to territorial jurisdiction, which was now discarded, from the claim to self-determination, which was reasserted. This new form of official nationalism was expressed in amendments to Articles two and three of the Irish Constitution, approved in the May 1998 referendum, which replaced the claim to territorial jurisdiction with an aspiration to 'unite all the people who share the territory of the island of Ireland, in all the diversity of their identities and traditions'.

There were parallel reorientations in Britain's official nationalism. Under Labour's Tony Blair, the British government sought to strengthen the UK's national unity by recognising and accommodating its multinational diversity (O'Dowd, 1998). This replaced defensive British nationalism with a more proactive version that interpreted sub-national autonomy and cross-border or supranational institutions such as the EU as opportunities rather than threats. This 'unity in diversity' model reflected a wider process of regionalisation in the European Union and saw the government become an active advocate of limited devolution for Wales and Scotland. In Northern Ireland, meanwhile, the government was willing to delete the claim to absolute Crown sovereignty and accept some limited cross-border confederalism through North–South institutions. Neither of these initiatives was seen as undermining the constitutional guarantee, which was reasserted at every opportunity. This process of reconfiguring nationalism was clearly demonstrated on the eve of the referendum on the Peace Agreement, when Blair and Trimble made a joint televised appeal for a 'yes' vote against a backdrop of five pledges handwritten by Blair. The first of these stated there would be 'no change in the status of Northern Ireland without the expressed consent of the people of Northern Ireland' and was followed by the assurance that 'whatever the result of the referendum, as Prime Minister of the UK, I will continue to work for stability and prosperity for all of the people of Northern Ireland'.[10] In this way the Agreement allowed political relations to be reconstituted rather than transformed. This was most clearly reflected in the reassertion of Britain's underlying majoritarian guarantee, which was now overlaid with a range of reciprocal and consensus-building frameworks.

Interpreting the Agreement

In discussing the power-sharing model floated in the 1995 Framework Document, Arend Lijphart, a long-time advocate of 'consociationalism' asserted that the proposed model was 'the very opposite of the majoritarian model of democracy to which the British cling for the government of Great Britain' (1996, p. 273). What Lijphart failed to mention was that the power-sharing approach was also the 'very opposite' of the constitutional foundation of Northern Ireland, namely the British guarantee that there would be no change in its constitutional status until a majority of Northern Ireland residents voted for it. Indeed, the eventual Peace Agreement can in part be seen as a consolidation of that guarantee – as an Agreement designed to maximise consent for the status quo rather than as one designed to supersede or transform it.

Despite these continuities the Peace Agreement did signal a significant turning point. It suggested a process of mutual recognition across the unionist–nationalist divide and offered the possibility of accommodation between British and Irish nationalism. The resulting mutual engagement has allowed significant adaptation as contending nationalisms have begun to interrelate in new ways, in what may be seen as the first step on a long journey. Engagement requires recognition of the legitimacy of contending political positions and leads to some mutual adaptation. This falls short of mutual transformation, and there is no leap into the 'post-nationalism' predicted for instance by Richard Kearney (1997). Nationalisms, whether in their Irish, British or unionist variants, are realigned and reproduced, not superseded by the process of EU integration.

This perspective is confirmed by Newsinger who argues that the 1998 Peace Agreement points to a 'reconstitution of the bourgeois order, not in the context of the British Empire as in 1920–22, but in the context of the European Union' (1998, p. 11). The new context reconfigures relations between 'cores' and 'peripheries' amongst the EU's member states, and in

Ireland it alters the meaning of North– South divisions and in some senses reverses them.

This book has highlighted the contingency of national division and is intended as a critique of Tom Nairn's hypothesis, discussed in this book's introduction, that uneven development provided a 'permanent' basis for separation between Northern Ireland and the Republic. Positing an Ireland of 'two nations' prevents analysis of the emerging dynamics of North–South relations and of the resulting redefinition of unionism and nationalism. It also ignores the possibilities of border-crossing, jurisdiction-bridging initiatives, that perhaps are the most significant outcomes of the Peace Agreement. In establishing North–South institutions, the two governments have signalled a willingness to permit a partial sharing of power, adapting themselves to growing transnational North–South integration in Ireland. This adaptation is open-ended, and is expected to gain its own dynamic; while confederal decision-making through North–South institutions is initially confined to economic policy-making, under the Agreement it can be extended to other areas of social and political life 'where there is mutual cross-border and all-island benefit'.

These institutional innovations have the potential to reconfigure the political landscape and could open up a deeper process of North–South democratisation and empowerment. Under the Agreement, involvement in North–South decision-making would be limited to officials and ministers from the Dáil and the new Northern Assembly. This could, and perhaps should, be extended to secure wider involvement and legitimacy. The many organisations working on a North–South basis, from business to campaigning and community organisations, could be given a role in North–South policy-making. This is hinted at in the Agreement's reference to 'an independent consultative forum, representative of civil society' and could be developed into an all-island advisory body, an island 'Social Forum' with direct input into North–South decision-making. The participatory input could also be strengthened through greater accountability to elected representatives, perhaps via a directly elected 'Parliamentary Forum' as a more effective alternative to the indirectly elected advisory body proposed under the Agreement. Such initiatives could strengthen the process of political interaction; interest mediation would occur in the Social Forum and cross-party brokerage could emerge in the Parliamentary Forum. Disagreements on cross-border and all-Ireland issues would overlay, disrupt and undermine disagreements on the national question and in the process, positive-sum political conflicts could begin to replace the zero-sum politics of national conflict (see Anderson and Goodman, 1998).

These frameworks for reconciliation are in many respects the product of strengthened reciprocal relationships between North and South in Ireland. The relationships have emerged out of the process of reversing uneven development in Ireland – a process that has intensified during the 'Peace Process'. In this respect, the Peace Agreement can been seen as a long overdue attempt at catching up with the reality of North–South convergence. By establishing a system of regulation for emerging linkages between North and South, it offers the possibility of overcoming uneven ideological and institutional development. In doing so, it offers the possibility of overcoming national conflict.

Notes

INTRODUCTION

1 Upper-case 'North' and 'South' are used when referring to post-Partition Ireland.

CHAPTER ONE

1 Central Statistical Office (CSO) Command Reports: (1873) *The Changing Hours and Rates of Pay in Textiles Factories*; (1893) *The Conditions of Work in Belfast Flax Mills and Linen Factories*; (1894) *The Labour of Women and Girls in Textile Factories*; (1912) *The Conditions of Employment in the Linen and Making-up Trades.*
2 There were similar expectations of a more sustained revival of overseas investment in the wake of the 1994 'peace process'; *Business Telegraph*, 16 August 1994.
3 Smyth, 1993, p.135–8; CSO *Regional Trends* (various years).
4 *Sunday Tribune*, 12 May 1992. Integrationism was also supported by the 'Friends of the Union' group which was set up by Ian Gow and other British Conservative MPs to oppose the Anglo–Irish Agreement of 1985 (see *The Untried Solution: a Stronger Union*, Friends of the Union Group, July 1993). The 'Campaign for Equal Citizenship', which wanted British political parties to organise in Northern Ireland, and was particularly active in the British Labour Party as the 'Campaign for Labour Representation in Northern Ireland', also had integrationist implications (see McNamara, (1993) *Oranges or Lemons, Should Labour Organise in Northern Ireland?* London; Campaign for Labour Representation in Northern Ireland (1987) *McNamara's Ban, Belfast).*
5 *Sunday Tribune*, 28 March 1993.
6 Tom Garvin, 'Long Division of the Irish Mind', *Irish Times*, 28 December 1993.
7 Ibid.
8 *Guardian*, 28 November 1992.
9 *Irish Times*, 6 June 1991, 1 April 1993, 26 August 1993.
10 Garret Fitzgerald writing in the *Belfast Newsletter*, 25 September 1993.

11 *Irish Times*, 30 December 1993.
12 *Irish Times*, 8 March and 16 June 1993.
13 See NIO (1972) *The Future of Northern Ireland: a Paper for Discussion*, HMSO, London.
14 Hansard (1976). House of Commons 912/1994, 11 September 1976.
15 Doyle, 1994; Bob Cooper, Chair of the Fair Employment Commission, writing in the *Belfast Telegraph*, 1 October 1993.
16 Northern Ireland's prison population was 110 detainees per 100,000 residents. The prison population for non-'terrorist' crime stood at 32 per 100,000; *Irish Times*, 16 October 1993.
17 In 1993, this request was granted by the Court, which concurred with the British government position that there existed a 'public emergency threatening the life of the nation'. This justified UK derogation from the requirement that suspects be brought 'promptly' to court. The Prevention of Terrorism Act, 1974 permitted seven days' interrogation of suspects, renewable by the Secretary of State, before being formally charged, *Financial Times*, 26 October 1991 and 27 April 1993.
18 *Irish Times*, 8 May 1993; *Guardian*, 26 July 1993.
19 *Irish News*, 2 April 1993; *Irish Times*, 28 May 1993.

CHAPTER TWO

1 Morrissey, M. (1993). The rise and rise of unemployment, speech to the conference on *Interregional Economic Development in Ireland, in an EC Context*, organised by the Socialist Group of the European Parliament at the Wellington Park Hotel, Belfast, 1993.
2 NESC, 1989; EP 1991, p. 28–9.
3 Whether using GDP or GNP based on current prices and exchange rates or on current prices and purchasing power standard (PPS), O'Cleireacain, 1983, p. 108. See also *Belfast Telegraph*, 8 June 1993; *Guardian*, 31 January 1994.
4 See Chapter One and Chapter Four.
5 For instance, there was a shift from non-cattle meat production (pork, chicken, eggs) to beef, veal and dairy production in the late 1970s and early 1980s to sixty-three per cent of total output value in Northern Ireland and seventy-five per cent in the Republic. See Cooperation North (1991) *Study of Farm Incomes in Northern Ireland and the Republic of Ireland*, Study Series 3, Report 1, Dublin and Belfast.
6 The funding threshold was seventy-five per cent of average EU per capita GDP. The 'special reasons' were never spelt out.
7 *Irish Times*, 3 May, 24 February 1993.
8 IDB Chair, speaking at a conference on *Interregional Economic Development in Ireland, in an EC context*, organised by the Socialist Group of the European Parliament at the Wellington Park Hotel, Belfast, 1993.

9   *Belfast Telegraph*, 8 June 1993; *Belfast Newsletter*, 4 February 1993.
10 Internal working document of Commission services: The Community Support Framework for Northern Ireland 1988–93, 12 June 1989.
11 Coopers and Lybrand, *Northern Ireland and 1992*, January 1990, p. 51.
12 Coopers and Lybrand, *Survey of Business Attitudes*, February 1992.
13 This was an observation made in several interviews carried out in the course of the research for this study. The Taoiseach was speaking as President of the EU during the Republic's Presidency of the Council of Ministers, *Financial Times*, 27 May 1990; *Agence Europe*, 13 April 1990.
14 Wilson R. (1990) Hurrah for Mr Haughey, *Fortnight* May 1990, 9–10; *Europe*, Newsletter of the EC in Belfast, May 1990.
15 *Irish Times*, 16 June 1992, also cited by the Irish Taoiseach in his introduction to DSO, 1992b.
16 *Irish Times*, 6 October 1989.
17 *Financial Times*, 23 December 1992.
18 George Quigley, Chair of the Institute of Directors, NICE, 1993, p. 128–9.
19 *Irish News*, 20 March 1992, *Belfast Newsletter*, 11 February 1992.
20 CBI (1992) *Priorities for European Structural Funding 1994–8: a Strategy for Accelerated Growth to Facilitate Economic and Social Convergence Within the EC*, 8 October 1992, Chapter Five: A joint North–South approach, p 20.
21 *Belfast Newsletter*, 11 February 1992.
22 A positive approach to the new Europe, *CBI News*, June 1992, p.6.
23 Nigel Smyth speaking at a conference on *Interregional Economic Development in Ireland, in an EC context*, organised by the Socialist Group of the EP at the Wellington Park Hotel, Belfast, 1993.
24 Stewart N. (1992) *Submission to Initiative '92*.
25 *Belfast Newsletter*, 1 February 1992, 9 February and 24 February 1993.
26 *Financial Times*, 29 November and 15 December 1993.
27 Freeman J. Gaffikin F. and Morrissey M. (1989) *The Irish Economies: a Common Future*, Belfast: ATGWU; Moriarty T. and Morrissey M. (1989) *The Economies in Ireland*, Belfast: MSF.
28 *Irish Times*, 20 December 1992.
29 Newsletter of the Northern Ireland Centre in Europe, 10 October 1992.
30 *Irish Times*, 26 March 1993; *Belfast Newsletter*, 13 March and 31 March 1992.
31 *Sunday Tribune*, 20 June 1993; *Irish Times*, 23 August 1993.
32 *Irish Times*, 16 June 1993.
33 *Irish Times*, 31 December 1993.
34 *Irish News*, 2 June 1992, 10 March and 16 May 1993.
35 *Irish Times*, 1 May 1992.
36 Sweeney P. (SIPTU), 'Economic development: a trade union response', in Shirlow P. (Ed.) *Development Ireland*, 69–81, Pluto: London. See also the 'Culliton Report', DSO, 1992a.

37 *Irish Times*, 20 March 1992.
38 *Irish News*, 30 March 1993; *Belfast Telegraph*, 3 March 1993.
39 *Independent on Sunday*, 12 December 1993.
40 This was reflected in migration patterns and holiday destinations as much as in socio-economic orientations: in 1993, one year after the completion of the SEM, South–North tourism fell by seventeen per cent, *Irish News*, 4 March 1993.
41 Labour costs were fifteen to twenty per cent lower in Northern Ireland. This was illustrated by a project funded by the EU under the 'STAR' programme which assisted in the installation of a £100 million fibre optic link-up with Britain, encouraging 'back-office locations' from the south-east of England into Northern Ireland. Private and public sector organisations, such as insurance companies, British Telecom directory enquiries, British Airways ticket sales, as well as DSS offices relocated to Northern Ireland to take advantage of labour market conditions, *CBI News*, June 1992; *Financial Times*, 30 April 1992.
42 *Irish Times*, 26 February 1993
43 K. Bloomfield, Northern Ireland Assembly, Minutes of evidence on the Anglo–Irish summit, Northern Ireland Assembly Reports, 28 November 1983; *Belfast Newsletter*, 18 May 1993; *Belfast Telegraph*, 5 October 1993.
44 Geoff MacEnroe, Director, North–South business development programme, CII/IBEC: 'Accelerating growth to facilitate economic and social cohesion within the EC', speech to the conference on *Interregional Economic Development in Ireland, in an EC Context*, organised by the Socialist Group of the European Parliament at the Wellington Park Hotel, Belfast, 1993.
45 *Financial Times*, 25 February 1993; *Irish Times*, 26 February 1993.
46 In 1990, EU expenditure in the Republic accounted for IR£1,306 million out of total public expenditure of IR£12,061 million; in Northern Ireland it accounted for St.£158 million out of a total public expenditure of St.£6,596 million. In 1995–6, Northern Ireland EU expenditure accounted for St.£187 million out of a total public expenditure of St.£7,737 million. See DFP(NI) (1994) *Northern Ireland expenditure plans and priorities, 1994–5*; NIEC 1992.
47 NIO Press Release, 27 July 1993.
48 *Belfast Newsletter*, 1 February 1992.
49 *Financial Times*, 4 October 1990.
50 *Irish Times*, 21 May 1992.
51 European Economy, 1994, p. 174, Tables 68 and 73. See also DSO, 1992a, p. 24.
52 *Belfast Telegraph*, 8 June 1993.
53 As Northern Ireland is part of the UK there are no trade statistics for the region. Estimates were made by the NIERC in its Report, *Exports of NI manufacturing Companies*, published in 1990.

Notes

1 Richard Kearney writing in the *Irish Times*, 5 May 1993; Boyle 1991, p. 69; similar sentiments were expressed in Kearney, 1988.

2 Logue H. (1992) *Submission to Initiative '92*.

3 Conlon B. (1990) Integrating: Europe, Ireland, *Fortnight* May 1990, 8–9.

4 Kearney R. and Wilson R. (1992) *Submission to Initiative '92*; *Irish Times*, 3 February 1992.

5 *Financial Times*, 16 November 1990.

6 He asked 'where is Northern Ireland?' – to be informed that the North had acceded to the 1973 treaties as the 'United Kingdom of Great Britain and Northern Ireland' while the Republic had acceded as 'Ireland', Official Journal, 23 October 1980, C275/21, Written Question 680/80.

7 In the space of four years in the 1980s there was a significant increase in the proportion of both communities identifying themselves as 'northern Irish', from 11 per cent to 16 per cent for Protestants and from 20 per cent to 25 per cent for Catholics, Moxon-Browne, 1991, p. 25–6.

8 In 1989 for instance, 'northern Irish' identity appealed to 27 per cent of Sinn Féin supporters, 24 per cent of SDLP supporters, 14 per cent of OUP and 10 per cent of DUP supporters, Moxon-Browne, 1991, p. 29.

9 *Irish Times*, 5 July 1993.

10 House of Commons, *Direct Elections to the European Parliament*, (Command Report 6768, April 1977). Also see Elliott, 1980.

11 This was partly due to the UUP decision to field two candidates in 1979 – John Taylor and Harry West, splitting the UUP vote, Smyth, 1987, p. 160.

12 *Irish Independent*, 14 October 1980; *Belfast Telegraph*, 18 September 1981; *Irish News*, 19 September 1984.

13 *Irish News*, 29 January 1992.

14 Journalists asking why the cooperative spirit at the EU level could not be extended to break the political deadlock in Northern Ireland were informed by the Rev. Paisley that this could only be done by the Province itself while John Hume argued that there was 'no point in SDLP-DUP deal as it would exclude the two central actors in the conflict' – Britain and the Republic; *Belfast Telegraph* and *Irish Times*, 20 February 1988.

15 *Ulster Newsletter*, 7 January 1992; *Irish News*, 4 March 1992.

16 *Marxism Today*, June 1991.

17 *Belfast Telegraph*, 2 June 1989.

18 Glen Barr, formerly of the UDA, *Belfast Telegraph*, 22 February 1993.

19 Molyneaux was part of a UUP 'get Britain out' campaign; *Irish Times*, 19 April 1975.

20 *Irish Times*, 13 February 1993; K. Maginnis MP, speech to the Cork Chamber of Commerce, reported in the *Irish Times*, 13 February 1993.

21 Cllr Raymond Ferguson (UUP) quoted in the *Belfast Telegraph*, 16 March 1993.

22 *Belfast Newsletter*, and *Irish Times*, 22 January 1993.

23 The *Blueprint* also carried an appendix received from 'three very prominent businessmen', which argued for 'arrangements for enabling both parts of the island to develop a partnership on matters of mutual interest, on the basis of full equality and without threat to Northern Ireland's position within the UK'. It was argued that 'if a relationship of mutual trust were progressively developed, we would expect such a partnership as it proved itself, to become increasingly close'.

24 Peter Robinson, DUP MP, quoted in *Financial Times*, 1 January 1992.

25 *Belfast Newsletter*, 4 June 1992.

26 *Eurobarometer*, Autumn 1992.

27 There was a seventy per cent turn out and seventeen per cent voted against membership; *Irish Times*, 28 April 1987.

28 Garret Fitzgerald, writing in the *Irish Times*, 14 September 1991.

29 *Belfast Telegraph*, 8 May 1990.

30 *Irish Times*, 24 May 1992.

31 *Irish Times*, 25 May 1992.

32 Cadogan Group (1994) *Blurred Vision: Joint Authority and the Northern Ireland Problem*, p. 17, CG: Belfast.

33 Cllr William Ross UUP and Seamus Mallon MP, SDLP deputy leader quoted in the *Irish Times*, 17 March 1993; John Taylor MP, UUP, *Guardian*, 8 December 1993.

34 From the UUP, John Taylor, *Belfast Newsletter*, 31 December 1992; from the DUP, Peter Robinson, *Irish Times*, 9 February 1993; the Rev. Paisley, *Financial Times*, 14 June 1989; and Cllr S. Wilson, *Irish Times*, 2 April 1993.

35 *Belfast Telegraph*, 15 September 1982.

36 *Irish News*, 12 March 1993.

37 *Financial Times*, 15 August 1988.

38 *Irish Times*, 10 February 1990; 19 November 1990.

39 *Irish Times*, 10 May 1993.

40 Dilating here refers to a process of expanding or widening. John Hume, *Subsidiarity and the Role of the Regions*, 9 December 1992, Edinburgh University.

41 *European*, 25–7 May 1990.

42 *SDLP Proposals to Government on the Preparations of the Community Support Framework, 1994–99*, March 1993.

43 John Hume speaking on *Northern Ireland: A Place Apart?* BBC Radio Four, 29 November 1992; *Sunday Tribune*, 8 November 1992.

44 *Irish Times*, 26 January 1993; 13 May 1992.

45 *Irish Times*, 24 February 1992.

46 *Irish Times*, 14 October 1993; *Guardian*, 7 December 1993; *Times* (London), 29 February 1994.

47 Mitchell McLaughlin, Northern Chair of Sinn Féin; *Guardian*, 5 April 1993.

48 The viewpoints here are drawn from *Northern Limits–The Boundaries of the Attainable in Northern Ireland Politics*, a publication of the unionist-orientated 'Cadogan Group', comprising A. Aughey, P. Bew, A. Green, D. Kennedy and P. Roche, p. 11–19, 1992.

49 *Irish News*, 6 October 1981; *Irish Times*, 3 May 1991; *Belfast Telegraph*, 10 June 1992; *Belfast Newsletter*, 9 April 1993.

50 As John Taylor argued in 1992; *Irish Times*, 16 June 1992.

51 *Irish Times*, 12 October 1992; *Irish News*, 20 October 1992; *Irish Times*, 2 February and 24 May 1993.

52 *Irish Times*, 13 July 1984; *Agence Europe*, 11 October 88; *Belfast Telegraph*, 12 October 1988; *Financial Times*, 4 January 1992.

53 DUP election material and *Irish News*, 31 May 1984; *Belfast Newsletter*, 12 November 1993.

54 See its submission to *Initiative '92* printed in *New Ulster Defender*, 1 April December 1992; *Guardian*, 17 January 1994.

55 *Irish Times*, 22 April 1991.

56 *Sunday Independent* opinion polls and *Irish News*, 14 April 1993.

57 In addition, forty-eight per cent saw a federal Republic and forty-two per cent saw a North–South federation as 'desirable'; *Irish Times*, 10 June 1992; *Irish News*, 16 June 1992.

58 *Financial Times*, 11 May 1990.

59 *Irish Times*, 27 November 1993.

60 *Sunday Press*, 1 November 1993.

61 Fitzgerald, 1962; these ideas were more fully developed in the early 1970s with the publication of Garret Fitzgerald's *Towards a New Ireland*, which stressed that the Republic's and Northern Ireland's membership of the EU 'may well prove to be the most important single factor influencing events in a positive direction [i.e. towards reunification] in the years ahead' (Fitzgerald 1972, p. 103).

62 Dáil debates 578, 9–8 May 1973.

63 Dáil debates, p. 1923, 21 March 1972, Motion on membership of EEC.

64 Speaking at the Anglo–American Press Association, Paris, 18 October, 1972, Department of Foreign Affairs, Statements and Speeches, 5/72.

65 *Irish Times*, 16 May 1987.

66 *Financial Times*, 22 January 1990.

67 NIF (1983) *Reports of Proceedings; Irish Times*, 20 November and 21 November 1989.

68 *Irish Times*, 12 May 1990.

69 *Irish Times*, 22 April 1991; *Agence Europe*, 14 March 1991.

70 *Irish Times*, 14 December 1990.

71 *Irish Times*, 8 April 1993; *Financial Times* and *Sunday Tribune*, 28 April 1993. Speech to the University College Dublin Law Society, 20 January 1994.

72 *Belfast Telegraph*, 26 November 1993.

73 *Irish Times*, 6 March 1993; the principles appeared to have popular support–as confirmed by an opinion poll *Irish Times*, 27 November 1993.

74 *Irish News*, 4 March 1993.
75 *Irish Independent*, 28 January 1983; NIF (1983) *Reports of Proceedings*.
76 *Financial Times*, 3 June 1989.
77 Chris O'Malley, Fine Gael MEP (1988) *Over in Europe*, Orchard Press, Dublin
78 *Irish Times*, 8 January 1993.

CHAPTER FOUR

1 *Independent on Sunday*, 13 June 1993; *Financial Times*, 10 January 1992.
2 Cochrane, 1993; *Financial Times*, 18 June 1993; *The Planner*, 27 November 1992.
3 The LGIB explicitly drew on the experience of other EU states in its campaign. See LGIB Press Releases, 20 July 1992 and 30 October 1992; House of Commons (1993) *The Maastricht Debate: The Committee of the Regions*, House of Commons Library Records Paper 93/9, 28 January 1993. See also Association of County Councils (ACC) 1992; *Local Government Chronicle*, 8 May 1992; *Guardian*, 9 March 1993.
4 *Municipal Review and AMA News*, March 1993, p. 266.
5 *Guardian*, 27 February 1992 and 2 March 1992; *Telegraph*, 5 March 1993.
6 HMSO (1992) *The Functions of Local Authorities in England*, Department of the Environment, Local Government Review. Examples include the North West Regional Association; SERPLAN South East Regional Planning Forum; West Midlands regional Forum; Yorkshire and Humberside Standing Conference; and East Midlands Regional Forum; the Western Development Partnership.
7 *Financial Times*, 5 November 1993.
8 HMSO (1993) *Scotland and the Union*, March 1993.
9 Laffan (1989); *Irish Times*, 28 October 1988; Statement to the Dáil by the Taoiseach in December 1988, DSO (1989) *Developments in the EC*, Report 33, 83, January 1989; *Irish Times*, 5 December 1988.
10 Tom Barrington, Director of the Institute for Public Administration, Dublin, writing in the *Irish Times*, 5 December 1988.
11 Most of the funds were channelled through the Department of Finance. Regional working groups had little access to the sectoral review groups at the national level. See Community Workers Cooperative, 1989, p. 3; also DSO (1991) *Developments in the EC*, 37, 55, January 1991.
12 Later there were complaints that the proposed regional bodies would not be directly elected; *Irish Times*, 8 January 1993.
13 *Irish Times*, 6, 7 and 8 April 1993; *Irish Times*, 2 June 1993.
14 Commission Vice President Tugendhat, speech delivered at Queen's University on the tenth anniversary of British and Irish membership of the Community, 25 January 1983.

15 Revealingly, it was felt that such measures were needed as 'stronger agreements' were required in an EU without internal borders; see European Parliament, 1982, p. 28–9.

16 European Parliament debates, Bangemann 1–312/165; the Report argued that Northern Ireland 'is, and always has been a constitutional oddity' – in terms of political sympathies, administration and political practice. European Parliament 1984; Hickman, 1990.

17 *Irish Times*, 17 October 1988; *Financial Times*, 17 August 1986 and 16 November 1990; *Agence Europe*, 4206, 18 November 85. See also Fitzgerald, 1991, p. 478 and Loughlin, 1991.

18 Guelke 1988, p. 162; Agreed Communique, September 1977, DSO.

19 *Irish Independent*, 16 November 1985.

20 As Lady Thatcher disclosed in her memoirs, 'the international dimension became easier to deal with'; *Irish Times*, 18 October 1993.

21 Gallagher, 1985; *Guardian*, 26 July 1993.

22 Speech to the IDB in Brussels, 23 June 1985.

23 Northern Ireland Information Service 26, 5 June 1985.

24 EP debates, 18 June 1981, commenting on the Martin Report Doc. 1–177/81.

25 EP debates, 29 March 1984, Paisley (Official Journal 1–312/168) and Catherwood (1–312/174); EP, 1984.

26 Regulation 1739/83, 21 June 1983; Official Journal, L171 29–26.

27 Official Journal, C117 30.4.84; EP 1986, *An Integrated Rural Development Programme for the Less favoured Areas of Northern Ireland*, the 'Maher Report', PE A2–105/86, 25 September 1986.

28 EP written question, 13 November 1986 (Official Journal, 2–345/197).

29 NIEC, 1992, Trimble, 1989b.

30 NIEC Report on Structural Funds, 1992; *Belfast Telegraph*, 21 September 1989.

31 *Agence Europe*, 7 February 1992; NIEC, 1992, p. 67.

32 The Republic successfully campaigned for the retention of dairy support within the CAP, in contrast with British government rejection of it. See O'Cleireacain, 1983, p. 124; NIF, 1984c, p. 67.

33 Resolution of 9 April 1981 arising from the Plumb Report Doc. 1–108/81. When the Republic won an extension of the 'suckler cow premium' in 1983 it was applied to both North and South, *Farmweek*, 14 September 1984; NESC/NIEC, 1988; DSO, 1992b, p. 92.

34 Written Questions, Official Journal C74/22, 12 November 1979; C144, p. 90, 15 June 1981; C149, p. 67, 14 June 1982.

35 *Irish News*, 13 December 1982.

36 *Irish News*, 13 October 1982.

37 'Europe' Newsletter of the Commission office in Northern Ireland, No. 68, May 1991; *Irish Times*, 3 November 1992.

38 *Anglo-Irish Joint Studies*, report presented by the Taoiseach, Dr Garret Fitzgerald, to the Oireachtas, DSO, 11 November 1989; See written questions, Official Journal, C226/38, 24 August 1987 and C295/15, 5 November 1987.

39 ECU 24 million was provided for the period 1981 to 1985 and ECU 16 million from 1985 to 1989, see Official Journal, C86/13, 8 April 1980; C1345/29, 3 June 1985; Regulations 2619/80 and 3637/85; *Agence Europe*, 16 May 1988 and 9 March 1989; Official Journal, 248/8, 30 September 1985.

40 Commission Regulation C1562/3, 25 July, 1991; *Joint INTERREG programme for Northern Ireland and Ireland 1991–3*, submitted to the EC Commission, 23 August 1991, p. 91; *European Information Service*, March 1993; Keating, 1991, p. 102.

41 This information is drawn from confidential interviews with Commission representatives. It was possible to estimate the Northern allocation at approximately £31.6 million, HMSO, 1993.

42 There was a new reference to the need for industrial development assistance for firms operating on an all-Ireland basis, HMSO, 1993, p. 112–26.

43 *Belfast Telegraph*, 10 June 1992; Eithne Fitzgerald, Minister of Finance, responsible for the NDP, 'Ireland in Europe – a shared challenge', speech to the conference on '*Interregional Economic Development in Ireland, in an EC Context*', organised by the Socialist Group of the European Parliament at the Wellington Park Hotel, Belfast, 1993; Donoghue, 1993, p. 19.

44 The North–South chapter appeared in the same form as in the NDP, DSO (1993); Dick Spring, Encounter/BIA, 1993, p. 25.

45 *Irish Times*, 12 October 1993.

46 *Irish Times*, 6 October 1989; *Telegraph*, 12 March 1992, special edition on Northern Ireland, 'North and South with one Purpose' by Chris Ryder.

47 *Irish Times*, 11 November 1978.

48 *Irish Times*, 5 June 1990 and 20 March 1992; *Irish News*, 20 March 1992.

49 See 'Regionalism and EC Trends' in *New Statesman and Society*, 6 December 1991 and *Economist*, 8 August 1992.

50 See House of Commons (1969) *The Redcliffe-Maud Commission into Local Government*, Command Paper 4040, CSO: London; *Guardian*, 21 June 1993; Gordon, 1990; Hayton, 1992; ACC, 1992; *Municipal Journal*, 7, 19 February 1993.

51 *Irish Times*, 10 March 1993; *Independent on Sunday*, 6 February 1994.

52 See *Northern Ireland Expenditure Plans and Priorities*, March 1994, DFP/Treasury; Knox, 1992.

53 *Financial Times*, 19 October 1992.

54 Institute for Public Policy Research (1991) *The Constitution of the UK*, Constitution Series, 1991–1993, Institute for Public Policy Research (IPPR) London; British Labour Party (1991) *Devolution and Democracy* BLP: London July 1991; Liberal Democratic Party (1992) *At the Heart of Our Democracy*, Policy Briefing 36, October 1991, LDP: London.

55 *Irish Times*, 12 May 1990.

56 *Irish Times*, 15 January 1991.

57 *Irish Times*, 11 November 1988; Sinnott, R. Regional Elites, Regional Powerlessness and the European Regional Programme in Ireland, in Leonardi (1992), 71–109; Hickman, 1990 and Walsh, 1995.

58 *Irish Times*, 15 February 1994; DSO, 1990.

59 See statements by the Permanent Secretary, Department of Finance and Personnel, and by the Reverend Beattie at a meeting on the Anglo–Irish summit, Northern Ireland Assembly, 28 November 1983, Minutes of Evidence, 14, 1283.

60 DSO 1992b; Keatinge, 1988, p. 102. See joint statement arising out of the Inter-Government Conference (IGG) of 21 October 1987.

61 Four years later this stipulation was strengthened by the European Parliament which emphasised that border regions should be able to 'conclude agreements, cooperate on any matters they consider to be of common interest and enter into direct relations with their neighbours across the border without requiring the power of delegation or any authorisation from their central governments'; EP, 1992b, p. 6; *Belfast Telegraph*, 31 July 1990; *Belfast Newsletter*, 1 February 1992. See also EC Regulation 2052/88.

62 *Irish Times*, 16 January 1993; *Independent*, 28 January 1993.

63 *Irish Times*, 22 July 1993; *Financial Times*, 17 December 1993.

64 British government communication to the IRA, said to be personally approved by the Secretary of State, dated 19 March 1993, reported in the *Belfast Newsletter*, 30 November 1993.

65 *Irish Times*, 15 September 1992 and 28 October 1992; *Ulster Newsletter*, 25 January 1993.

66 *Irish Times*, 6 April 1993; *Ulster Newsletter*, 4 February 1993.

67 *Belfast Telegraph*, 13 September 1993; *Guardian*, 18 February 1994.

68 *Financial Times*, 16 December 1993.

69 *Belfast Telegraph*, 29 October 1993.

70 *Scotsman*, 24 January 1994; *Irish Times*, 2 February 1994.

71 *Irish Times*, 24 February 1994.

72 *Financial Times*, 2 August 1993.

73 The Labour Party was committed to promoting 'national reconciliation and unification in Ireland', while the Conservative Party remained formally committed to maintaining the 'Union' as an end in itself. See Composite 44, Agreed at the Labour Party Conference, Brighton, September 1993. This was underlined with the publication of unofficial Labour proposals for 'joint responsibility' between the Republic and the UK for the administration of Northern Ireland; *Irish Times*, 2 July 1993.

74 *Belfast Newsletter*, 23 July 1993; *Financial Times*, 2 July 1993; *Irish Times*, 15 July 1993; *Financial Times*, 18 March 1993.

75 *Irish Times*, 22 October 1988; *Financial Times*, 26 October 1991; NIO (1994) *Northern Ireland Expenditure Surveys*, 1994–5 and 1991–2, NIO: Belfast.

76 *Financial Times*, 16 December 1993.

77 *Financial Times*, 16 December 1993.

78 *Irish Times*, 13 February 1993.

79 *Irish Times,* 12 February 1993.
80 *Irish Times,* 30 January 1993, 11, 12 and 16 February 1993.
81 *Financial Times,* 20 June 1990; *Irish Times,* 13 June 1990; *Belfast Telegraph,* 8 June 1993.
82 *Irish Times,* 12 February 1993.
83 Statement of the Taoiseach, Charles Haughey, *Developments in the European Communities,* Report to the Dáil, 39, 124, 12 December 1991, following the conclusion of the IGC of 9 December 1991 that approved the Maastricht Treaty.
84 *Irish Times,* 2 August 1993; *Financial Times,* 1 February 1993.
85 *Irish Times,* 3 February 1993; *Guardian,* 5 February 1993.
86 In a speech in Paris, *Irish Times,* 11 February 1993.
87 *Irish Times,* 1 February 1993; *Financial Times,* 6 October 1992.
88 *Irish Times,* 21 March 1993.
89 *Sunday Tribune,* 7 February 1993.
90 *Irish Times,* 12 October 1993.
91 *Belfast Telegraph,* 26 November 1993.
92 *Irish Times,* 29 November 1993.
93 There was a remarkable consensus in the press that the declaration had redefined 'Britishness'; *Daily Telegraph,* 18 December 1993; *The Times,* 21 December 1993; *Guardian,* 23 December 1993; *Belfast Telegraph,* 23 December 1993.

CONCLUSIONS

1 *Irish Times,* 3 October 1998.
2 *Irish Times,* 25 November 1998.
3 *Irish Times,* 29 April 1998
4 The Republic's 'Operation Matador' was launched in April 1996. The Garda were joined by twenty-two mobile army patrols in September 1996. In the same month the three Northern Ireland MEPs and the Ulster Farmers' Union visited the British Prime Minister in an attempt to classify Northern beef as non-British. The ban on Northern Ireland beef was not lifted until October 1997; see *Irish Times,* 24 April and 19 September 1996; 3 October 1998.
5 'Weak NI economy needs South link', Garret Fitzgerald, *Irish Times,* 28 November 1998.
6 *Irish Times,* 29 May 1998; *Belfast Telegraph,* 18 April 1998.
7 *Irish Times,* 18 April 1998; *Belfast Telegraph,* 21 April 1998.
8 Robert McCartney, UK Unionist Party, *Belfast Telegraph,* 21 May 1998; Ian Paisley, DUP, 16 May 1998; Peter Robinson, DUP, 14 May 1998.
9 *Irish Times,* 14 February 1996.
10 *Irish Times,* 21 May 1998.

Bibliography

Amin, S. (1980) *Class and Nation*, Translated by S. Kaplov, Monthly Review Press: New York.

Anderson, J. (1994) Problems of interstate economic integration: Northern Ireland and the Irish Republic in the Single European Market, *Political Geography*, 13, 1, 53–73.

Anderson, J. and Goodman, J. (1993) European integration and the national conflict in Ireland, in King R. (Ed.), *Ireland, Europe and the Single Market: Geographical Perspectives*, Geography Society of Ireland Special Publications, No. 8, 16–30, GSI: Dublin.

Anderson, J. and Goodman, J. (1994a) European and Irish integration: contradictions of regionalism and nationalism, *European Journal of Urban and Regional Studies*, 1, 1, 49–62.

Anderson, J. and Goodman, J. (1994b) Northern Ireland: dependency, class and cross-border integration in the European Union, *Capital and Class*, 54, 13–25.

Anderson, J. and Goodman, J. (1995a) Euroregionalism and national conflict: the UK, Ireland, North and South, in Shirlow P. (Ed.) *Development Ireland*, 39–54, Pluto: London.

Anderson, J. and Goodman, J. (1995b) Regions, states and the European Union: Modernist reaction or postmodernist adaptation? with James Anderson, *Review of International Political Economy*, 2, 3, 600–632.

Anderson, J. and Goodman, J. (1998) *Dis/Agreeing Ireland: Contexts, Obstacles, Hopes*, Pluto Press. London.

Anderson, J. and Shuttleworth, I. (1993) Currency of cooperation, and bordering on the difficult, *Fortnight*, December–January, 286–287.

Armstrong, J. (1951) Social and economic conditions in the Belfast Linen industry 1950–1900, *Irish Historical Studies*, 3, 28.

Arthur, P. (1985) Anglo-Irish Relations and the Northern Ireland Problem, *Irish Studies in International Affairs*, 2, 1, 37–51.

Association of County Councils (1992) *The New Europe: Implications for UK Local Government*, ACC and Coopers Lybrand Deloitte, Paper 7, February 1992, ACC: London.

177

Audit Commission (1991) *A Rough Guide to Europe: Local Authorities and the European Communities*, HMSO: London.

Barooah, V. (1993) Northern Ireland: typology of a regional economy, in Teague P. (Ed.) *The economy of Northern Ireland*, 1–24, Lawrence and Wishart: London.

Bell, G. (1987) *The Protestants of Ulster*, Pluto: London.

Bell, P. (1993) Political and constitutional development in Northern Ireland in the context of a developing Europe, in Skar H. and Lydersen B. (Eds.) *Northern Ireland: a Crucial Test for a Europe of Peaceful Regions?* Norwegian Institute of International Affairs, 24–34, NIIA: Oslo.

Berresford Ellis, P. (1988) *James Connolly, Selected Writings*, Pluto: London.

Bew, P. et al. (1979) *The State in Northern Ireland 1921–72*, Manchester University Press: Manchester.

Blackwell, J. and O'Malley, E. (1983) EEC membership and Irish industry, in Drudy P. and McAleese D. (Eds.) *Ireland and the EC*, Irish Studies, 3, 107–143, Cambridge University Press/ Putman Press: Bath.

Bogdanor, V. (1992) *Local Democracy and the EC – Challenge and Opportunity*, Belgrave Papers, Number 6, Local Government Management Board: London.

Boserup, A. (1972) Contradictions and struggles in Northern Ireland, *Socialist Register*, 157–92.

Boyce, G. (1993) Ethnicity versus nationalism in Britain and Ireland, in Kruger, P. (Ed.) *Ethnicity and Nationalism: Case Studies in their Intrinsic Tension and Political Dynamics*, Deutsche Biblioteck, Hitzeroth: Marburg, Germany.

Boyle, K. and Hadden, T. (1994) *Northern Ireland: the Choice*, Penguin: London.

Bradley, J. and Whelan, K. (1992) Irish experience of monetary linkages with the UK and developments since joining the EMS, in Barrell R. (Ed.) *Economic convergence and Monetary Union in Europe*, 121–143, NESC/Sage: London.

Bradley J. et al. (1993) *Stabilisation and Growth on the EC Periphery*, Economic and Social Research Institute, Avebury: Aldershot.

Buckland, P. (1973) *Irish Unionism: Ulster Unionism and the Origins of Northern Ireland 1886–1922*, Gill and Macmillan: Dublin.

Clulow, R. and Teague, P. (1993) Governance structure and economic performance, in Teague P. (Ed.) *The Economy of Northern Ireland: Perspectives for Structural Change*, 121–141, Lawrence and Wishart: London.

Coakley, J. (1983) The European dimension of Irish public opinion 1972–82 in Coombes D. (Ed.) *Ireland and the European Communities*, 43–67, Gill and Macmillan: Dublin.

Cochrane, A. (1993) Beyond the Nation State? – Building the Euro-Region, in Bullmann U. (Ed.) *Die Politik der dritten Ebene Regionen im Prozess der EG – Integ*, Nomos: Nomos.

Commission of the European Communities (1990) *The Regions of the Enlarged Community: Periodic Report on the Social and Economic Situation and Development of the Regions of the Community*, Office of the Official Publications of the EU: Luxemburg.

Community Workers Cooperative (1989) *Whose plan? Community Groups and the National Development Plan*, November 1989, CWC: Dublin.

Connolly, M. (1992) Learning from Northern Ireland: an acceptable model for regional and local government, *Public Policy and Administration*, 7, 1, Spring 1992, 31–46.

Cormack, R. and Osborne, R. (1994) The evolution of a Catholic middle class, in Guelke A. (Ed.) *New Perspectives on the Northern Ireland Conflict*, 65–85, Avebury: Aldershot.

Coughlan, A. (1992) Northern Ireland: conflicts of sovereignty, *Studies: an Irish Quarterly review*, 81, 322, 180–190.

Cox, M. (1998) 'Cinderella at the Ball': Explaining the End of the War in Northern Ireland, *Millennium*, 27, 2, 325–42.

Cox, R. (1987) *Production, Power and World Order*, Columbia University Press: New York.

Crick, B. (1991) The English and the British, in Crick B. (Ed.) *National Identities*, Political Quarterly Special Edition, Blackwell: London.

Cullen, L. (1972) *An Economic History of Northern Ireland since 1660*, Batsford: London.

Department of Finance and Personnel (1992) *The Structural Funds in Northern Ireland after 1993*, conference papers, December 1992, DFP/Northern Ireland Centre in Europe: Belfast.

Derby, J. (1993) Regionalisation, new allegiances and identification in Northern Ireland and Europe, in Skar H. and Lydersen B. (Eds.) *Northern Ireland: A Crucial Test for a Europe of Peaceful Regions?* 40–49, Norwegian Institute of International Affairs, Foreign Policy Studies, 40, 54–65, NIIA: Oslo.

Ditch, J. and Morrissey, M. (1992) Northern Ireland: review and prospects for social policy, *Social Policy and Administration*, 26, 1, March 1992, 18–39.

Donoghue, D. (1993) Territorial claims and Ireland in a European context, in Skar H. and Lydersen B. (Eds.) *Northern Ireland: A Crucial Test for a Europe of Peaceful Regions?* Norwegian Institute of International Affairs, 40, 14–23, NIIA: Oslo.

Doyle, J. (1994) *The Failure of State Action in a Conflict Situation: the Case of Fair Employment in Northern Ireland*, paper presented at the Sociological Association of Ireland annual conference, May 1994, Derry.

DSO (1988) *National Development Plan, 1988–1993*, DSO: Dublin.

DSO (1990) *Local Government and Reform*, Report of the Advisory Expert Committee, the 'Barrington Report', DSO: Dublin.

DSO (1992a) *Report of the Industrial Policy Review Group*, the 'Culliton Report', DSO: Dublin.

DSO (1992b) *Ireland in Europe: A Shared Challenge, Economic Cooperation on the Island of Ireland in an Integrated Europe*, DSO: Dublin.

DSO (1992c) *Treaty on European Union*, White Paper on the Maastricht Treaty, April 1992, DSO: Dublin.

DSO (1993) *National Development Plan, 1994–1999*, DSO: Dublin.

Elliott, S. (1980) *Northern Ireland: The First Elections to the European Parliament*, Queens University: Belfast.

Elliott, S. (1990) The 1989 election to the European Parliament in Northern Ireland, *Irish Political Studies*, 5, 93–100.

Encounter and the British-Irish Association (1993) *Europe and its Regions After 1993 – Are We Being Left Behind?* Report of a conference at St Anne's College Oxford, April 1993.

European Dialogue (1993) *Power to the People? Economic Self Determination and the Regions*, Conference Report, Roberts A. (Ed.) European Dialogue/Freidrich Ebert Foundation: London

European Parliament (1979) *The Effects on Ireland of Membership of the European Communities*, Directorate General for research and documentation, non-official document prepared for the Socialist Group, PE 43.006/rev, Luxemburg.

European Parliament (1982) *The European Judicial Areas (Extradition)*, Report drawn up on behalf of the Legal affairs committee, 1–318/82, 14 June 1982, Luxemburg.

European Parliament (1984) *Report drawn up on behalf of the Political Affairs Committee on the Situation in Northern Ireland*, the 'Haagerrup Report', Parliamentary Working Documents, 1983–4, 1–1526/83, March 1984, Luxemburg.

European Parliament (1987) *Report on Behalf of the Committee on Regional Policy and Regional Planning – The Regional Problems of Ireland,* the 'Hume Report', A2 – 109/87, July 1987, Luxembourg.

European Parliament (1991) *The Impact of 1992 and Associated Legislation on the Less Favoured Regions of the EC*, Regional and Transport Series No. 18, EN.9.91, Luxemburg.

Farrell, M. (1976) *Northern Ireland: the Orange State*, Pluto: London.

Farrell, M. (1983) *Arming the Protestants: The Formation of the Ulster Special Constabulary and the Royal Ulster Constabulary, 1920–27*, Pluto: London.

Fenn, N. (1989) Britain, Ireland and European integration in Keogh D. Ed *Ireland and the Challenge of Europe*, 47–63, Hibernia University Press: Cork.

Fisk, R. (1975) *The Point of No Return*, Andre Deutsch: London.

Fitzgerald, G. (1962) The political implications of Irish membership of the European Communities, *Studies*, 51, 44–81.

Fitzgerald, G. (1972) *Towards a New Ireland*, Charles Knight: London.

Fitzgerald, G. (1991) *All in a Life: An Autobiography*, Macmillan: London.

Foley, A. and Mulreany, M. (1990) Conclusions, in Foley A. and Mulreany M. (Eds.) *The Single European Market and the Irish Economy*, 432–443, Institute of Public Administration: Dublin.

Fothergill, S. and Guy, N. (1990) Case Study: Northern Ireland, in Fothergill, S. and Guy, N. (Eds.) *Retreat from the Regions*, 138–159, Jessica Kingsley: London.

Gallagher, T. (1985) Anglo-Irish relations in the EC, *Irish Studies in International Affairs*, 2, 1, 425–453.

Gallagher, M. (1990) Do Ulster Unionists have the Right to Self-Determination?, *Irish Political Studies*, 5, 11–30.

Gibbon, P. (1975) *The Origins of Ulster Unionism: The Formation of Popular Protestant Politics and Ideology in Nineteenth Century Ireland*, Manchester University Press: Manchester.

Gillespie P. et al. (1992) *Maastricht – Crisis of Confidence*, Interim report, Institute of European Affairs: Dublin.

Goldring, M. (1991) *Belfast – from Loyalty to Rebellion*, Laurence and Wishart: London

Goodman, J. (1991) *Northern Ireland – the Reproduction of Capital or the Reproduction of Sectarianism?*, Middlesex Polytechnic, MA Dissertation.

Goodman, J. (1995a) *The Northern Ireland Question and European Politics*, in Catterall P. (Ed.) *Northern Ireland in British politics*, Institute of Contemporary British History and Macmillan: London.

Goodman, J. (1995b) Single Market and a Single Ireland, *European Brief*, 2, 6, 18–19

Goodman, J. and Pauly, L. (1993) The obsolesence of capital controls? economic management in an age of global markets, *World Politics*, 46, 50–82.

Goodman, J. (1996) *Nationalism and Transnationalism*, Avebury: Aldershot

Goodman, J. (1998) The Republic of Ireland: Towards a Cosmopolitan Nationalism?, in Anderston, J. and Goodman, J.,

Dis/Agreeing Ireland: Contexts, Obstacles, Hopes, Pluto Press: London.

Gordon, I. (1990) Regional Policies and National Politics in Britain, *Environment and Planning, Government and Politics*, 8, 427–38.

Graham, D. (1992) Tearing the house down: religion and employment in the Northern Ireland housing executive, in Stewart P. (Ed.) *Ireland's Histories: Aspects of State, Society and Ideology*, 129–149, Routledge: London.

Gramsci, A. (1971) *Selections from Prison Notebooks*, Lawrence and Wishart: London.

Guelke, A. (1988) *Northern Ireland: The International Perspective*, Gill and Macmillan: Dublin.

Habermas, J. (1976) *Legitimation Crisis*, Heinemann: London.

Hainsworth, P. (1981) Northern Ireland: A European Role? *Journal of Common Market Studies*, 20, 1, 1–15.

Hainsworth, P. (1992) Business as usual: the European election in Northern Ireland in Hainsworth P. (Ed.) *Breaking and Preserving the Mould: the Third Direct Elections to the European Parliament (1989) – the Irish Republic and Northern Ireland*, 143–161, Policy Research Institute: Belfast.

Hainsworth, P. and Morrow, D. (1993) *Northern Ireland: European region – European problem?* paper delivered at a conference on 'peripheral regions in the EU' organised by the Department of Sociology and the ESRC at Queen's University, Belfast, April 1993.

Hamilton, D. (1993) Foreign investment and industrial development in Northern Ireland, in Teague P. (Ed.) *The Economy of Northern Ireland: Perspectives for Structural Change*, 190–217, Lawrence and Wishart: London.

Harbinson, J. (1973) *The Ulster Unionist Party 1882–1973: its Development and Organisation*, Blackstaff: Belfast.

Harrison, R. (1990) Northern Ireland and the Republic of Ireland in the Single Market, in Foley A. and Mulreany M. (Eds) *The Single European Market and the Irish Economy*, 406–443, Institute of Public Administration: Dublin.

Hart, M. and Harrison, R. (1992) Northern Ireland, in Martin R. and Townroe P. (Eds.) *Regional Development in the 1990s*, 117–127, Regional Studies Association, Jessica Kingsley: London.

Hayton K. (1992) *Local Economic Development and Scottish Local Government Reform*, November 1992, The Planning Exchange: Manchester.

Hazelkorn, E. and Patterson, H. (1994) The new politics of the Irish Republic, *New Left Review*, 207, 49–72.

Hickman, M. (1990) *Ireland in the European Community*, European Dossier Series, 19, Polytechnic of North London Press: London.

Higgins, M. (1992) Ireland in Europe 1992, in Kearney R. (Ed.) *Across the Frontiers*, 58–77, Wolfhound: Dublin.

HMSO (1993) *Northern Ireland Structural Funds Plan 1993–1999*, HMSO: Belfast.

HMSO (1994) *Single Programming Document 1994–1999*, HMSO: Belfast.

Hunt, M. (1981) *British Labour History 1815–1914*, Weidenfeld and Nicolson: London.

Jay, R. (1989) Nationalism, Federalism and Ireland, in Jay R. (Ed.) *Nationalism, federalism and Ireland*, 209–249, Centre for Federal Studies, Leicester University Press: Leicester.

Kearney, R. (1997) *Post-nationalist Ireland: Politics, Culture and Philosophy*, Routledge: London.

Kearney, R. (1988) *Across the Frontiers: Ireland in the 1990s*, Wolfhound: Dublin

Keatinge, P. (1991) Foreign Policy, in Keatinge P. (Ed.) *Ireland and EC Membership Evaluated*, 147– 164, Pinter: London.

Kennedy, K. et al. (1988) *The Economic Development of Ireland in the Twentieth Century*, Routledge: London.

Knox, C. (1992) Community relations: the role of local government in Northern Ireland, *Local government policy making*, 19, 2, October 1992, 29–35.

Laffan, B. (1983) The consequences for Irish Foreign Policy, in Coombes D. (Ed.) *Ireland and the European Communities*, 89–110, Gill and Macmillan: Dublin.

Lee, J. (1973) *The Modernisation of Irish society 1848–1918*, Gill and Macmillan: Dublin.

Leonardi, I. et al. (1992) The Regions and the European Community: the Regional response to the Single Market in the Underdeveloped areas, *Regional Politics and Policy – An International Journal*, Special Issue, 2, 1.

Lijphart, A. (1996) The Framework Document on Northern Ireland and the Theory of Power-Sharing, *Government and Opposition*, 31, 3, Summer 1996, 267–274.

Loughlin, P. (1991) The Anglo-Irish Agreement: Federal Arrangement or affirmation of the Nation-State? in *Federalisme*, 3, 183–197.

Lyne, T. (1990) Ireland, Northern Ireland and 1992: the barriers to technocratic anti-partitionism, *Public Administration*, 68, Winter 1990, 417–433.

Mackay, R. (1992) 1992 and relations with the EC, in Martin, R. and Townroe, P. (Eds.) *Regional Development in the 1990s – The*

British Isles in Transition, 278–87, Jessica Kingsley/Regional Studies Association: London.

Mansergh, N. (1981) The influence of the past, in Watts D, (Ed.) *The Constitution of Northern Ireland*, National Institute of economic and social affairs, Joint studies in public policy, 4, 5–25, Heinemann: London.

Matthews, A. (1994) *Managing the EU Structural Funds*, Undercurrents, 5, Cork University Press: Cork.

Millar, D. (1978) *Queen's Rebels: Ulster Loyalism in Historical Perspective*, Gill and Macmillan: Dublin.

Mitchell, A. (1974) *Labour in Irish Politics 1890–1930*, Dublin University Press: Dublin.

Mjoset, L. (1993) *The Irish Economy in Comparative Institutional Perspective*, National Economic and Social Council: Dublin.

Moxon-Browne, E. (1991) National identity in Northern Ireland, in Stringer P. and Robinson D. (Eds.) *Social Attitudes in Northern Ireland*, 1990–1991 edition, 23–31, Blackstaff press: Belfast.

Munck, R. (1993) *The Irish Economy: Results and Prospects*, Pluto: London.

Murray, A. (1903) *A History of the Commercial Relations between the UK and Ireland from the period of the Restoration*, London.

Murray, D. and O'Neill, J. (1991) *Peace building in a Political impasse: cross-border links in Ireland*, University of Ulster Centre for the Study of Conflict: Coleraine.

Murray, P. (1992) The European Parliament and the Irish dimension, in Hainsworth P. (Ed.) *Breaking and Preserving the Mould: the Third Direct Elections to the European Parliament (1989) – the Irish Republic and Northern Ireland*, 15–49, Policy Research Institute: Belfast.

Nairn, T. (1977) *The Break-up of Britain: Crisis and Neo-nationalism*, New Left Books: London.

Nairn, T. (1997) *Faces of Nationalism: Janus Revisited*, Verso: London.

National Economic and Social Council (1983) *Review of Industrial Policy*, National Economic and Social Council Report, 64, the 'Telesis Report', NESC: Dublin.

National Economic and Social Council and Northern Ireland Economic Council (1988) *Economic Implications for Northern Ireland and the Republic of Ireland of Recent Developments in the EC*, jointly published in Dublin and Belfast.

National Economic and Social Council (1989) *Ireland in the European Community: Performance, Prospects and Strategy*, National Economic and Social Council: Dublin.

New Ireland Forum (NIF) (1984a) *The Macroeconomic Consequences of Integrated Economic Policy, Planning and Co-ordination of Ireland*, prepared by McCarthy Ltd, N. Gibson and D. McAleese, DSO: Dublin.

New Ireland Forum (NIF) (1984b) *Final Report*, DSO: Dublin.

New Ireland Forum (NIF) (1984c) *An Analysis of Agricultural Developments in the North and South of Ireland and of the Effects of Integrated Policy and Planning*, NIF sectoral studies, May 1984, DSO: Dublin.

Newsinger, J. (1998) The Reconstruction of Bourgeois Order in Northern Ireland, *Monthly Review*, 50, 2, June 1998, 1–11.

Northern Ireland Centre in Europe (NICE) (1993) *Network Europe: Strategies for European Interregional Partnerships*, conference proceedings, October 1993, European centre for regional development/Northern Ireland centre in Europe: Belfast.

Northern Ireland Economic Council (NIEC) (1982) *The Financial System in Northern Ireland*, report number 29, April 1982, NIEC: Belfast.

Northern Ireland Economic Council (NIEC) (1989) *Economic Assessment*, report number 75, April 1989, NIEC: Belfast.

Northern Ireland Economic Council (NIEC) (1990) *Economic Assessment*, report number 81, April 1990, NIEC: Belfast.

Northern Ireland Economic Council (NIEC) (1992) *The EC Structural Funds and Northern Ireland*, Belfast: NIEC.

Northern Ireland Office (NIO) (1972) *The Future of Northern Ireland: A Paper for Discussion*, HMSO: London.

O'Brien, M. (1993) Ireland and the EC: past performance and future prospects, in Cooney J. and McGarry T. (Eds.), *Post-Maastricht Europe*, papers from the 1992 Humbert Summer School, 139–153, Humbert Publications: Dublin.

O'Cleireacain, S. (1983) *Northern Ireland and Irish Integration: the Role of the European Communities*, Journal of Common Market Studies, 22, 2, 107–124.

O'Donnell, R. (1991) Identifying the issues, The regional issue, in O'Donnell R. (Ed.) *Economic and Monetary Union*, Studies in Monetary Union, 2, 1–47, 87–139, Institute of European Affairs: Dublin.

O'Donnell, R. (1993a) *Ireland in Europe: Challenges for a New Century*, Economic and Social Research Institute: Dublin.

O'Donnell, R. (1993b) Ireland and Europe: the Political, Economic and Cultural Dimensions, in *Ireland, Europe and the Single Market*, King R. (Ed.) Geographical Society of Ireland, Special Publications, No. 8, 1–15, Trinity College, Dublin.

O'Dowd, L. (1980a) Shaping and reshaping the Orange state, in O'Dowd, L. et al. (Eds.), *Between Civil Rights and Civil War*, CSE Books: London.

O'Dowd, L. (1980b) Regional Policy, in O'Dowd, L. et al. (Eds.), *Between Civil Rights and Civil War*, CSE Books: London.

O'Dowd, L. (1998) Constituting Division, Impeding Agreement, the Neglected Role of British Nationalism, in Anderson, J. and Goodman, J. (Eds.) *Dis/Agreeing Ireland: Contexts, Obstacles, Hopes*, Pluto Press: London.

O'Dowd, L. and Corrigan, J. (1992) *National Sovereignty and Cross-border Cooperation: Ireland in a Comparative Context*, Sociological Association of Ireland Annual Conference, Cork, 8–10 May 1992.

O'Dowd, L., Corrigan, J. and Moore, T. (1993) Borders, national sovereignty and European integration: the British– Irish case, *International Journal of Urban and Regional Research*, 19, 2, 272–85.

OECD (1985) *Ireland, Economic Survey*, April 1985, OECD: Paris.

OECD (1991) *Ireland, Economic Survey*, April 1985, OECD: Paris.

O'Hearn, D. (1993) Global competition, European and Irish peripherality, *Economic and Social Review*, 24, 2, 169–197.

O'Hearn, D. (1998) *Inside the Celtic tiger: the Irish Economy and the Asian Model*, Pluto Press; London.

O'Leary, B. (1990) Party support in Northern Ireland 1969–1989, in O'Leary, B. and McGarry, J. (Eds.) *The Future of Northern Ireland*, 342–357, Clarendon: London.

O'Leary, B. and Arthur, P. (1990) Northern Ireland as a site of nation-building failures, in O'Leary, B. and McGarry, J. (Eds.) *The Future of Northern Ireland*, 1–48, Clarendon: London.

O'Leary, B. and McGarry, J. (1990) Northern Ireland: options, a framework and analysis in O'Leary, B. and McGarry, J. (Eds.) *The Future of Northern Ireland*, 270–290, Clarendon: London.

O'Malley, P. (1993) Reinterpreting Northern Ireland, in O'Maolain C. (Ed.), *Register of Research on Northern Ireland*, foreword, i–viii.

O'Malley, P. (1985) Industrial Development in the North and South of Ireland: Prospects for an Integrated Approach, *Administration*, 33, 1, 61–85.

Patterson, H. (1980) *Class Conflict and Sectarianism: the Protestant Working Class and the Belfast Labour Movement 1869–1920*, Blackstaff: Belfast.

Pringle, D. (1985) *One island, Two Nations? A Political Geographical Analysis of the National Conflict in Ireland*, Research Studies Press: Letchworth.

Probert, B. (1978) *Beyond Orange and Green: The Political Economy of the Northern Ireland Crisis*, Zed: London.

Quigley, G. (1992) *Ireland – An Island Economy*, text of speech to the Confederation of Irish Industry, February 1992, Dublin.

Riordan, R. (1920) *Modern Irish Agriculture and Industry*, Metheun: London.

Rolston, B. (1987) Reformism and sectarianism: the state of the union after civil rights, in Darby, J. (Ed.) *Northern Ireland: the Background the Conflict*, 197–224, Appletree: London.

Rolston, R. (1991) Containment and its Failure: The British State and the control of conflict in Northern Ireland, in George, A. (Ed.) *Western State Terrorism*, 155–180, Routledge: New York.

Rose, E. (1992) A Europe of regions – the West Midlands of England: planning for metropolitan change in Birmingham, *Landscape and Urban Planning*, 22, 229–242.

Rosebaum, S. (Ed.) (1912) *Against Home Rule: the Case for the Union*, London.

Rowthorn, R. and Wayne, N. (1988) *Northern Ireland: The Political Economy of Conflict*, Polity: London.

Ruane, J. and Todd, J. (1991) Why Can't You Get Along With Each Other? in Hughes, E. (Ed.) *Culture and Politics in Northern Ireland 1960–90*, 27–43, Taylor and Francis and Open University Press: London.

Ruane, J. and Todd, J. (1992a) Ireland: North and South and European integration in Hainsworth, P. (Ed.) *Breaking and Preserving the Mould: the Third Direct Elections to the European Parliament (1989) – the Irish Republic and Northern Ireland*, 163–192, Policy Research Institute: Belfast.

Ruane, J. and Todd, J. (1992b) The social origins of nationalism in a contested region: the case of Northern Ireland, in Coakley, J. (Ed.), *The Social Origins of National Movements*, 187–212, Sage: London.

Rumpf, M. and Hepburn, J. (1977) *Nationalism and Socialism in Twentieth Century Ireland*, Liverpool University Press: Liverpool.

Scott, A. and Millar, D. (1992) *Subsidiarity and the Scottish Dimension – A Discussion Paper*, presented to the Europe of the Regions Conference, Edinburgh, November 1992.

Smyth, C. (1987) *Ian Paisley: the Voice of Ulster*, Scottish Academic Press: Edinburgh.

Smyth, M. (1993) The public sector and the economy, in Teague, P. (Ed.), *The Economy of Northern Ireland: Perspectives for Structural Change*, 121–141, Lawrence and Wishart: London.

Solow, B. (1971) *The Land Question and the Irish Economy 1870–1903*, Harvard University Press: London.

Stormont, (1957) *An Economic Survey of Northern Ireland*, the 'Isles and Cuthbert Report', HMSO: Belfast.

Stormont, (1962) *Report of the Joint Working Party on the Economy of Northern Ireland*, the 'Hall Report', HMSO: Belfast.

Stormont (1964) *The Economy of Northern Ireland*, the 'Wilson Report', HMSO: Belfast.

Strauss, E. (1951) *Irish Nationalism and British Democracy*, Metheun: London.

Temple-Lange, J. (1988) The Draft Treaty on European Union and the member states: Ireland, in Beiber, R. et al. (Eds.) *An Ever Closer Union: A Critical Analysis of the Draft Treaty Establishing European Union*, European Perspectives Series, 241–259, European Commission: Brussels.

Todd, J. (1987) Two traditions in Unionist political culture, *Irish Political Studies*, 1, 1–26.

Trimble, M. (1989a) The European Community and Northern Ireland, in Hainsworth, P. and Trimble, M. (Eds.), *Northern Ireland in the EC*, 93–114, Policy Research Institute: Belfast.

Trimble, M. (1989b) The regional policy of the EC, in Hainsworth, P. and Trimble, M. (Eds.), *Northern Ireland in the EC*, Policy Research Institute: Belfast.

Walsh, F. (1979) The changing industrial structures of Northern and Southern Ireland, *The Maynooth Review*, 5, 2, 3–14.

Walsh, J. (1995) EC structural funds and economic development in the Republic of Ireland, in Shirlow P. (Ed.) *Development Ireland*, 54–69, Pluto Press: London.

Ward, M. (1991) The women's movement in the north of Ireland, in Hutton, S. and Stewart, P. (Eds.) *Ireland's Histories – Aspects of State, Society and Ideology*, 149–163, Routledge: London.

Whyte, J. (1983) The permeability of the United Kingdom-Irish border: a preliminary discussion, *Administration*, 31, 3, 300–15.

Whyte, J. (1991) *Interpreting Northern Ireland*, Clarendon: Oxford.

Index

Index

Index